47 Eureka solutions to life's biggest problems

Wendy Churchill & Rebecca Ash

JUST ONE MINUTE

47 Eureka solutions to life's biggest problems

Wendy Churchill & Rebecca Ash

Wendy Churchill & Rebecca Ash
Design: Matt Lawrence

Published 2008 by Oxfordshire Press Ltd

Oxfordshire Press Ltd
Emery House
Unit 7-9 Romsey Industrial Estate
Greatbridge Road
Romsey SO51 OAD
www.oxoxpress.com

Tel: 0845 0727 380

ISBN: 978-0-9557324-2-3

CONTENTS

Your Health and Longevity 115

Important note

The publishers have carefully checked the contents of *How to change your life in JUST ONE MINUTE* to ensure that it's as accurate as possible at the time of publication.

That said, please be advised that the information in these pages is not necessarily representative of health professionals and physicians. Please don't treat it as a substitute for medical advice from qualified doctors.

If you are pregnant, we advise that you seek professional advice before making any dietary changes.

You should seek medical attention in all emergencies, such as accidents, high fever or heart attack. If you are worried that you have a serious illness, please consult a medical professional first.

This book is here to educate. Neither the author nor the publishers can accept legal responsibility for any problems that may occur with trying the ideas, tips and recommendations in this book.

This book is dedicated to all the readers of *Life is a Bag of Revels.*
Thank you for your great support over the years.

About the authors

Wendy Churchill is the author of *Life is a Bag of Revels*, the popular free e-column read by some 25,000 people every week. If you haven't already discovered the delights of Wendy's wonderful musings on life, health, happiness and worldly wisdom, Wendy welcomes you to join her community of subscribers by visiting her website at **www.bagofrevels.co.uk.**

Rebecca Ash is a freelance copywriter and author of *The New Spend Less Handbook - 365 Tips for a Better Quality of Life While Actually Spending Less.*

Introduction

Introduction

From Wendy Churchill

Being born with a human mind is like being sold a car without being told where the brakes are, how the gears work – or that it's wonderful on a sunny day to drive with the windows open...

By the time we leave school and reach adulthood, most of us have been taught how to read a poem, multiply a fraction, and place the Industrial Revolution accurately on a time scale. Unfortunately, such knowledge – while obviously mind-expanding and essential for passing exams – has done very little to prepare us for the challenges of actually *being*.

As we go on our journey through life, we are pretty much left to teach ourselves how to think, how to live, or how to respond to life's problems. Yes – we are taught useful things like mathematics, changing a light bulb, and baking a sponge cake. But who teaches us the right way to act when we find that we do not like our job? Is it right, wrong or even normal to rate and compare ourselves against others around us? How we can cope with the way we get so anxious when we walk into a room full of strangers?

In the early years of our life we all tend to chose ways to think and act through guesswork. Habit and copying the people around us also play their part. Later on, as we stumble across certain books or ideas – or we have sudden eurekas of understanding – we realise that some of the habits or reactions we have developed are unhelpful. They're faulty or sometimes even downright destructive. Worse still, many of these destructive ways of behaving, we find, are practiced by almost everyone else around us.

The majority of people are suffering so much, but there are so many ways of living life better

All the "Eurekas" you will read about in this book have had an enormous impact on our own lives – providing the kind of instructions about how to live that we often seem to be lacking. Each has left us either more sane, more calm, more positive, more confident, more healthy, more successful, more pleasant, or better equipped for living life *well*. I would even go as far as to say that they have made us happier.

With some of the eureka discoveries I have made myself, I have almost been infuriated. Infuriated at the idea that I had not been told about this before and that most human beings remain ignorant of something so useful. Indeed, being born with a human mind is like being sold a car without being told where the brakes are, how to fill up the water for the windscreen or that on a sunny day it's wonderful to drive with the windows open.

This book is our attempt to share with as many people as possible the eurekas that we have been lucky enough to stumble across in our own lives so far – so that more of us can drive along with the windows open in the sunshine. Few of them are new or original. Most have been handed down in different forms by throughout the centuries. But the more people who discover them – and the more even those who already know them are reminded of them again – the better, we believe, this world will be.

Life is an ongoing learning, unlearning and re-learning process and we are, I believe, slowly progressing in the right direction. There are many people who say (and I am wont to do this myself) that we are not in a good place right now – because we are too materialistic, too disconnected from the spiritual, and overanxious. But human beings have always been anxious, always been materialistic… always in the process of changing. And is it not a case of three steps forward, one step backward?

This book is not so much about improving who you are, but improving your ability to truly be that person. To live up to your full potential. To give life your best shot. And to feel happier in your skin.

How to Use this Book

From Rebecca Ash

How small changes in the way you live, think and act can have an enormous impact on your entire life

Yet it is sometimes those tiny changes that can take the greatest leaps of faith and determined persistence to execute

A few weeks ago, my daughter announced that she wanted to learn how to tie her shoelaces.

"Okay," I said, bending down to untie my own shoes and offer her a demonstration. But by the time I got to the bit about "wrapping this other lace around the loop and *doing this*," I realised what an amazingly complicated thing it is that I normally do without even thinking.

"Doing this," I thought, was going to take a bit of practice to get the hang of.

If my daughter was going to learn how to tie her shoe laces it was going to take more than one demonstration, a lot of persistence, and a lot of practice before it would eventually come naturally. And it is often the same for learning the new habits of living, doing or thinking that some of the eurekas in this book demand.

Right now, you have probably been employing most of your habits of thought and action for a large part of your life. Unlearning some of those habits, therefore, may take some undoing. If you start feeling anxious and nervous even at the thought of attending a social event or making a phone call, for example, then it's going to take practice and persistence to learn a *new* way of reacting to this event. But just like learning to tie your shoe laces, it will eventually come naturally to you.

We act and feel along the same neural pathways – just as a record always plays the same tune along the grooves

Whenever we get into a certain habit of acting, reacting or thinking, what has happened is that set neural pathways have been made in our brains between some of the billions of brain cells it contains. Our reactions to life become fixed in automatic patterns – in the same way that the traffic between London and Birmingham always comes up the M40. And our various views of life, our opinions about ourselves, and our emotional habits, are as solid and set as the concrete beneath it.

Another way of looking at neural pathways is to see them as ruts – rather like the ruts that sheep make as they repeatedly follow the same route across a hill… or an ancient bridleway that goes down between two banks, sinking deeper and deeper between them as the centuries pass.

Discovering some of the eurekas in this book, we hope, will be like suddenly realising that you can actually climb up onto one of those banks – and discovering what a wonderful view you have across the fields and valley from up there. But it will still take some time before it becomes more automatic to walk along the bright bank than to follow your normal trodden path along the dark rut below.

With some of the eurekas in this book, a change will happen instantly for you as you read it – or you'll instantly be set off down a path towards a new habit, a new goal or a new challenge. For some of the eurekas, however, you may find that you will need to work on this new habit, repeating the action persistently and consciously until eventually a new rut or neural pathway has been created. Progress may even seem slow, at first, and there will sometimes be set backs or complete or partial relapses.

The important thing is persistence and repetition – another reason why we have chosen to set out this book in short little "eurekas" that you can keep coming back to for reminders. We have discovered from our own experience that even those eurekas that seemed so miraculous when we first discovered them, can sometimes get quickly lost as we immerse ourselves back in to the all-consuming, sometimes blinding challenge and unstoppable business of our lives. Not to mention the old habits of being which are instantly easy to slip back into.

Our hope is that this book will be something you can return to time and time again for little nudges in the right direction… for a little space or time for reflection… or for those times in your life when you need a little extra support, direction or guidance.

Your Life and Your Relationships

Eureka No. 1

You can make almost ANYTHING you want happen in your life – simply by deciding that it WILL happen

Chance is all well and good and many great things happen to us through luck alone. If you're wishing for something specific to happen in your life, however, then leaving it to chance is not your best strategy.

You will not become a politician or a doctor or even a nurse or counsellor, for example, unless you make the decision that you want that to happen. Without that decision and the actions that follow, there is very little chance that your life will take that path. Make that decision, however, and there is a very good chance that the wheels you set in motion will start leading you towards your goal.

We all have far more ability to make things happen in our own life than we ever normally realise or are willing to take responsibility for. Perhaps through a lack of self-belief or a belief that this is not how our life was meant to be, we can tend to bemoan what we never get instead of really striving to make it happen.

If there is something you really want to happen in your life, then today is the day you can start making it happen. Before you do proceed, however, there are two questions you need to ask yourself. If you answer 'no' to either of them then you may need to do some more thinking.

1. **Is this the kind of thing that I can make happen myself?** If you're hoping to win the lottery, for example, then there's very little you can do to arrange for that yourself. If you're wanting to find a partner then obviously there's a lot more you can actually do to make that happen than crossing your fingers on a Saturday night.

2. **Do I REALLY want this to happen?** It is a strange quirk of human nature that we can sometimes spend a lot of time

wishing for something which isn't exactly what we want. Perhaps it has become a short cut for something else we might want but haven't yet put our finger on. Only when it comes to deciding that you're actually going to make something happen, does it really become important to know *exactly* what that is.

Once you have made the decision that you really want to make something happen then the next two things you need are CONVICTION and a PLAN.

First of all, you need to make the decision that this is something that you are DEFINITELY going to make happen in your life. If you take the attitude that you're hoping this is something that *might* happen then you've immediately lost your new power and your chances of achieving your goal go way down.

Secondly, you need to make a PLAN to make it happen. You must work on your plan. And you must give it time.

How much time? Well, how about two years?

I know it sounds strange to be so specific about the time but there is something very important about the two-year period. Basically, we all massively overestimate how much we can achieve in two months, but underestimate how much we can achieve in two years.

Whether your aim is to write a novel, change your career, double the amount you earn… become a new and improved person, make a patchwork quilt… or create a vegetable garden… one of your most important ingredients for actually making it happen could be giving yourself two years in which to do it.

The next thing you have to do is get the ball rolling. Two years doesn't mean you can slack off! The idea here is to carry out just small steps towards your goal – but steps which set things moving in a way that makes it difficult not to continue. If your goal was to write a novel, for example, you could book yourself into a creative writing course. If your goal is to find a new partner then your first small but brave step might be to put an advert in a lonely hearts column.

Few things will happen unless you take steps to make them happen yet many of us live our lives as if we believe that chance will do it all for us. Simply sitting at home dreaming or wishing is a very ineffective way of getting things to happen!

Eureka No.2

You are probably living your whole life according to a 'script' you wrote as a child

Here's your chance to rewrite it for the better and get rid of restrictions, blockages and destructive life influences...

If you believed as a child that your life was going to be good and that you'd be successful but not too successful, then there's a good chance that your beliefs have become reality. If you felt that you were always going to be victimised, pushed down or miserable, then that has more likely become your fate.

The life decisions you made as a child have probably even had an enormous influence on factors ranging from the number of kids you have and the kind of car that you drive through to your relationship with money and whether or not you judge yourself too harshly.

This is one of the key ideas in the Transactional Analysis school of psychotherapy – that most people live their whole lives according to a set of rules, ideas and character types that they wrote for themselves in response to their experiences and treatment during childhood. These can include such specific details as "Nobody will ever notice how good I really am," "I only get attention when I'm being bad," and "If I act all cute and pretty Daddy will give me a hug or some money."

Take, for example, a child who was born into a large family. Unable to easily get anybody's attention for himself, this child decided early on that the best policy was to go off on their own and look after and entertain themselves. As an adult this chosen behaviour may be positive in as much as this person is able to be on their own and be self-sufficient. On the downside, it might also mean that this person still shuns company when in fact more contact with others could make them much happier. This person may feel unable to approach people already formed in groups. They may also feel that they are not important enough for other people to pay them any attention.

Or how about a child brought up by a mother who was very down and depressed at home but who put on a bright and happy face in public. They might grow up to believe that that is how *everybody* is, and conform to this way of being themselves. A child who is told (explicitly or implicitly) that they are 'hopeless', 'bad', 'stupid' or 'pretty but dumb' may grow up to play that role they have been given.

Of course, it is certainly possible for people to have experiences later on in life which help to alter these habits and beliefs that they have. But it is also amazing how someone can go through their whole life believing that the view formed in childhood is actually the TRUTH – and therefore be unable to even realise that they could choose to have a different view if they wanted to.

A nice phrase that Transactional Analysis has for this phenomenon is the idea of a Life Script. Thanks to the experiences that we have in our formative years, we make decisions about how our life is going to be in the future. Then, as if we had written the story of our life before it started, we live out our lives according to the rules we have written for it.

Which of these 'opinions' about life could be tainting your every living moment?

Our individual life scripts may include, for example, some of these recognised and often common components:

People are not to be trusted.

Life is boring.

Life is great. Even if I feel terrible I should pretend I am happy.

I will always be unhappy.

I shouldn't show or even have any emotions.

I need to be loved by everyone around me, or I will feel unhappy and lonely.

It will be my job to be a mother and I am not able to be anything other than that.

When I need money, I have to ask a man to give it to me.

It is never a good idea to get close to other people.

Once I get to a certain point with anything, I don't know what to do with myself next.

I'm not allowed to have fun.

I can't have fun until I've finished my work.

Life is terrible. Everything that happens to me is terrible.

I can never get what I want most.

I've made my bed, now I have to lie in it.

I can have fun today, but I'll have to pay for it tomorrow.

I'm not a great person.

I am no good.

I am the kind of person who will almost make it but not quite.

And so on and so on. I'm sure you can add some very poignant scripts of your own.

Of course, we all have a lot of positive elements in our scripts as well. But those, quite simply, are not the ones we need to change.

We do NOT have to live out our lives as a lesser person because that was what we decided at the age of five. One does NOT have to continue thinking life is always awful simply because that is a habit you were raised into. And we do NOT have to go on believing that we are shy, useless, unlovable or whatever it is that we see as our negative points.

Change, of course, is never easy. To change the person you are can take a great leap of faith and some dedicated thinking and soul searching. We can also be very resistant to the idea of changing the kind of person we are, because in many ways we have become proud of our identity – even if it is damaging our lives.

A good place to start is to ask yourself questions about why you might have ended up with the characteristics and life script that you have today.

Ask yourself now...

What does the way I act in social situations say about me?
What did my experiences from childhood lead me to think about life?
What did my experiences from childhood lead me to think about myself and my position in life?

Remember, the things that you have come to believe about yourself and about your life are not the truth but rather a very powerful opinion. By changing what you think and believe you really can change your life. The world is not how it is but how you have come to view it.

Eureka No. 3

Dwelling on our problems encourages them to stay

Concentrating on the positive attracts good things into our life

Known as 'The Law of Attraction', 'The Secret', and the power of 'Positive Thinking', this Eureka can work in two different ways:

To attract something into your life you need to concentrate your thoughts on it.

To rid yourself of any problem, you need to avoid thinking about it – or concentrate instead on an opposite.

Take somebody trying to lose weight, for example. All day long they may be thinking of NOT eating but all they want to do because of that is eat. A person who spends all their time thinking about how depressed they are will have a hard time being anything else. The things that are most central in our mind are the things that we attract to our life, even if we are thinking that we wish things were different.

On the other hand, a person who has healthy thoughts about food will probably end up eating a healthy diet. A person who thinks of happy things and marvels at the joy of being alive this minute is very unlikely to be depressed. And a person who thinks positively about the wonderful job they know they're going to find soon will probably find one.

Of course, harnessing the power of this force can sometimes take quite a concerted effort. Recently, for example, I have been suffering from another bout of persistent headaches. While I was getting quite far in reducing them by pinpointing the kind of state of mind or semi-conscious thoughts that would often lead to them, I was still unable to rid myself of the problem. Then one day it suddenly struck me: the very fact that I was spending half the day concentrating on trying NOT to allow myself to develop a headache, was actually making headaches appear.

The power of your thoughts attract whatever you're thinking about into your life

Whenever we find ourselves in a situation we do not want to be in, it is often our human nature to spend a lot of time and energy dwelling on our dislike of the situation and our wish to escape it. Almost as if we are stuck in the groove of a rather depressing record, we go over and over the same points constantly, *wishing* it could be otherwise, but not actually doing anything about it. (Often, we're fooling ourselves that if we think about it some more we will be able to solve it.) Rather cruelly, unfortunately, it is just this kind of dwelling on our problems that keeps them in our lives.

- If you really want things to change, you've got to concentrate your mental energy on the idea of the positive change you need happening in your life.
- If you want something good to happen in your life, spend time every day having *positive* thoughts about that thing really happening.
- If you want to get away from something negative, think about its opposite and banish thoughts of the negative from your mind.
- If you want to be more confident, keep playing images of yourself in your head acting more confidently.
- If you want to stop eating chocolate but really can't stop thinking about it, start perhaps by seeing a picture in your mind's eye of one delicious small chocolate instead of a whole packet of Jaffa cakes.

The power of your thoughts can make amazing things happen in your life, rather like the way a placebo medicine can make your body heal itself. Try thinking about the word 'energy' without feeling at least a little bit energised. Try thinking about a lemon without your mouth watering.

Think about the words you want to tell yourself carefully, then repeat them to yourself whenever the reverse idea or thoughts come into your head. At first it will feel false and you don't think it will work. But then slowly you'll realise that it is beginning to work and the words are sinking in and melting in with the stuff of your mind.

Eureka No. 4

3 easy steps to solving any problem or unpleasant situation

And it all starts with an understanding of our human nature...

We human beings are very good at moaning about our problems – both to ourselves and to others. We are so good at moaning and bemoaning, in fact, that we actually start mistaking our lamenting for trying to *do* something about it.

It is almost, sometimes, as if we are blind to the possibility that our problem may be solvable, so tied up are we in it. We mistake our lamenting for taking action and therefore fail to change anything.

There are several possible reasons for this. Firstly, we are sometimes 'stuck in' or addicted to things being bad, because that is what we know – or even who we are. It is difficult to start imagining things being different. But only when we can start imagining what a solution might look like can we start working towards it.

A second major factor is that human beings generally dislike change. Sometimes making even the smallest move towards change can be a terrifying, paralysing thought. In some ways, in fact, it is a question of 'better the devil you know' than the fear we have of the new or the unknown.

Another factor that can stop us from taking action is our preference for feeling like the victim of the situation. Because it is something that is happening *to us*, we do not feel that we can do anything about it.

And finally, of course, we may simply *not know* what we might be able to do to try and solve our problem.

The following three easy steps offer a path to moving beyond procrastination and actually taking this problem by the horns.

1. Start first by WRITING DOWN what your problem is

Write out the whole list of problems if there is more than one. Chances are that, while you've probably been spending a lot of time with this problem inside your head, it may take on quite a different guise when you get it into the light of the real world and put it down on paper.

Left to the ever-present, all-evading, and yet outside the normal sphere of life existence they normally enjoy, one of the key characteristics of such problems is their insolvability. Problems immediately become a lot more solvable or manageable when written down on paper or on a computer file.

2. Take responsibility for the problem or the situation you're in

Take a look at the way you describe your problem, for example, to see to what extent you put yourself *in control* of it. Do you say "I" as the person who's doing at least part of the problematic something in the situation, or would you rather put the blame on the whole wide world, your mother, the colour of your hair or your star sign instead of admitting that you might have some input, responsibility or control over the situation?

The terrible truth, unfortunately, is that whenever we have some kind of problem situation, we normally play at least a part in creating that situation or allowing it to remain. In order to solve our problems, therefore, we have to accept some responsibility for them.

If you wrote down "Everybody is horrible to me" as your problem, for example, you will find it hard to change your situation unless you admit that something about your own behaviour must be partly responsible for this situation. You will not change all the everybodies. You can only change yourself. An alternative, therefore, might be along the lines of "Something about me allows others to he horrible to me" or "I always feel that other people are horrible to me".

Similarly, if you say that your problem is that "I've never had a lucky break", what you've got to realise is that lucky breaks don't get on a train from London to come and knock on your door. At the most they will travel from one desk to another or from you to a person standing next to you. You've got to put yourself in both the right place and frame of mind to get one.

3. Think of some actions you can start taking to solve the problem

Whatever the problem or uncomfortable situation you're in, it's more likely to get solved if you DO something to solve it yourself – rather than waiting for that Boeing 747 to land on top of your boss, your Lottery numbers to come up, or a letter to arrive on your doorstep carrying the answer to your problem.

Here are a few ideas to get you started:

- **Do some research** – Try a search on Google, take a trip to the library or buy a book on the subject. Your local branch of Citizens Advice Bureau may be able to help. Look for local or online support groups.
- **Talk to other people** – If, for example, you've got a problem with a teething baby, mice infestation or aphids on your roses, chances are that somebody you know will have had this problem before and be able to offer you advice. Beware, however, of talking to friends about problems like relationships or other deeper issues where they may sway you in a direction you don't necessarily want to go.
- **If the issue is a tricky one to act on**, explore how you really feel and what is perhaps holding you back. How? By answering questions on a piece of paper that you'd like to put to yourself – questions such as: What are all the different things you FEEL about this situation? What exactly is your thinking on this? Or go forward in time ten years, and look back at your current situation from that viewpoint…
- **Give yourself some small tasks** to actually DO. You can start with just small things at first. But it is essential to make sure that you are actually DOING something and being brave enough where necessary to carry out your planned action. Make a list NOW of things you can do.

Eureka No. 5

Want to be more confident and assertive?

Then the first thing you need to be is KIND

Shyness or social anxiety after the age of 20 is unnecessary and unjustified. It is actually much easier, in fact, to free yourself of this bad habit – which many of us have suffered – and become an adult.

Anxiety of any form is a phobia to life. But what is there really to be frightened of? After all, wouldn't it be nice to be one of those people who can always pick up the phone or walk up confidently to *anyone* without wanting to shrivel up, postpone it to another day, or trip over your words as if they were clinging on for dear life to your fillings.

The surprising key to all of this is to aim foremost to be NICE to the other people you need to communicate with or be with. Far from being the terrifying alien wearing a human mask that part of our inner fear seems to think that they are, see them as another human being just like you – with all the internal vulnerabilities and insecurities that you have.

Be the person who points out to the bus driver (politely) that he stops too far away from the curb for the old lady. *Be the person* who realises that the person they're thinking of phoning is just another human being and relishes the chance to make real contact with them.

Talk slowly, with kindness and purpose, and carry on talking 'till you've finished what you've got to say. Do not act as if you feel inferior to the person you're talking to – or as if they are not worth talking to.

Use confident body language by standing up straight and look the other person in the eye. Don't hunch your shoulders or look sheepish or shy. Talk in a relaxed and calm manner with open hands, open eyes and a smile.

The only way to really shine as the wonderful person that you are is not to worry about the way you are presenting yourself but just relax into being you. Dare to allow people to see all the things in you that you might be ashamed of, and you just might find that these are things they end up loving you most for…

Eureka No. 6

The next two minutes could change your relationship with your loved ones forever

Why we totally underestimate the emotional lives of those we spend most time with

It's amazing how little we actually know about what goes on inside the minds and inner lives of those around us. Next time you spot your nearest and dearest in the kitchen, take a good look at them and think about what they're thinking.

What is going on behind that face which you know so well? If you could listen in on their thoughts, what would they be like? Would you be shocked to find them very different to your own – or shocked to find them very similar? Would they be full of more vulnerability and strong emotion than you expected – or would you be shocked to find that their one all-consuming thought was a desire to become prime minister?!

To quote the great humanist psychotherapist, Carl Rogers, "Individuals have discovered in their closest friends and family members great realms of hidden feelings. There are previously unknown fears, feelings of inadequacy, suppressed rages and resentments, bizarre sexual desires and fantasies, hidden pools of hopes and dreams, of joys and dreads, of creative urges and unbidden loves."

Yet how many of us treat those around us with any understanding of the full extent of their humanness?

What is going on in the mind of the other person right now?

So often in our work and in our lives, we hear people complaining about the behaviour of others. Always that complaint is focused inside the life and mind of the complainer. Very little thought is given to attempting to understand where the behaviour of the other is coming from. Very little thought is given to what it is like to be inside their mind right now.

We often take the actions or behaviour of other people very personally, as an affront to ourselves. While in fact, those actions and behaviour are often so much more to do with what is going on inside the other person's mind, and not personally directed to you.

I am not saying that we should just put up with the bad behaviour of others and become either pushovers or super-human forgivers. Only that life could be richer, more rewarding, if you take some of the focus off your own inner feelings and try to focus simultaneously on the inner minds of others.

A family, it has been said, is only ever as happy as the least happy member of it. I think that can also be true of many relationships as well. It is quite likely that you are not going to have a particularly happy relationship with somebody who is not happy, or who has problems, or is suffering inside.

So what can we do?

We can listen a lot more and blame a little less. We can love, forgive and cherish more – even when it is hard to do.

When you are having issues with people you live or work with, spend a few minutes thinking about who they really are, where they're coming from, and what life might be like inside their head. Ask yourself questions like: What do they feel vulnerable about? What is motivating them to act in the way that they are in this situation? The more we try to understand, forgive and see it through the eyes of the other, the easier their behaviour will be for us to deal with.

If you really want to learn to see things from another's point of view (and this should, perhaps, be a compulsory activity when it comes to somebody we're married to) try putting pen to paper and writing a script as if you were that person. Imagine being that person and sitting down and writing a description of yourself or a short autobiography.

Eureka No. 7

An understanding of the 4 Basic Personality Types can revolutionise your relationships and dealings with others

It will also help you understand yourself better and work on your own strengths and weaknesses

Why are there some people in life who never get round to doing those urgent DIY jobs – while others are never happier than when fixing the sink or clearing the guttering? Why are some people chatty and friendly while others skulk in the background wishing they weren't there?

Over 2,400 years ago, the Greek physician Hippocrates first put together a theory of four different personality types. It goes a long way towards offering quite startling answers for just such questions. He named the four types Phlegmatic, Choleric, Sanguine and Melancholic – and he believed that we could be predominantly one or the other, or a mixture of two or more.

While you may find the idea of such personality types quite rigid at first, it can give you some very helpful insights into your own strengths, weaknesses and personality, as well as increased understanding of why some people act, think and feel so differently from you – and are sometimes even infuriating.

An understanding of the four temperaments can even ***help us find fondness for people we couldn't tolerate before... deepened love and forgiveness for our friends and family... and new inspiration to fulfill our true potential.***

Here below is a brief description of the four temperament types. Each person may be predominantly one, or a combination of several.

The Goal-Orientated Choleric: The Choleric person is active and quick. Enthusiastic, excitable and dynamic, they react strongly – and these impressions and reactions stay with them for a long time. They are proud and self-confident, aspire to great things and have the intelligence, strength of will and application to achieve.

The Goal-Orientated Choleric is a born leader, passionate and bossy, hardworking and always in haste. Good at organising, sometimes too impetuous, they are too proud to see their own weaknesses or to seek the help or advice of others. The Choleric tends not to have a very high opinion of others and doesn't have a great need for friends. Can be prone to anger. May alienate others and or make them feel insecure. Not prone to getting too upset or sad. Optimistic and full of energy. Doesn't spend much time relaxing. Hard rather than soft hearted. Finds it difficult to tolerate sickness and weakness in others. If she or he sets her or his will on changing, they have a high chance of succeeding. Goal and success orientated.

The Fun-Orientated Sanguine: The Sanguine character is easily aroused and passionate but moves on quickly to the next emotion or next reaction, the new thing of interest. They may also change opinions very quickly and easily. Their point of focus tends to be on the external rather than internal within themselves.

Vivacious and very talkative, they're fun to be with. Friendly and warm, but perhaps a little fickle. Doesn't like to be alone. All five senses are very active. The Sanguine person perhaps even thinks with senses rather than reason. They are optimistic. Can be quite vain and susceptible to flattery. Quick to get intimate but not always to love deeply. Prone to be lead into naughty behaviour. More likely to have an affair and be dragged into petty emotions such as envy. If their attempts to achieve things fail it may be because their optimistic outlook has prevented them from foreseeing obstacles – or their tendency not to dig much below the surface means they haven't examined the situation deeply. Happy to talk about and reveal themselves in the way that the Choleric or Melancholic isn't. Fun-orientated.

The Deep Melancholic: The Melancholic has a very internal, introverted and reflective personality. Thinks and feels deeply, yet is unlikely to show depth of emotion on the surface. In fact, an initial reaction to events or interactions may be slow in coming, but it will stay and run deep. Tends to be creative, poetic and philosophical. Very sensitive to the beauty of nature, ideals and the human predicament. May be highly perfectionist and meticulous about methods and details.

The Melancholic is neat and tidy and doesn't like to spend money.

Prone to sadness and depression and can have a poor self image. Can dwell on the dark or negative side of things – but also be overwhelmed with poetic awe and sympathy. May procrastinate and be indecisive and fearful of new undertakings. Reserved and not good at making new friends. Can be slow in talking and thinking – because he likes to reflect on things first. Can achieve great things if they push past their fear of failure and shame, and urge themselves forward.

The Easy-Going Phlegmatic: The phlegmatic isn't strongly interested in or reactive to what goes on around him. While he prefers rest and leisure to work, he does not – on the other hand – demand much of life or those around him either. He is therefore easy going and remains generally very composed and practical. Patient and sympathetic with others and rarely upset or emotional. Quietly witty. Enjoys eating and drinking. A steady but not particularly ambitious worker. Can be seen as lazy and doesn't like change. May put up with things for years but then suddenly snap. A more passionate and active person may get easily frustrated with having a phlegmatic as a partner. He or she, however, will be pretty good at putting up with anybody!

Eureka No. 8

You can make your life so much more exciting and eventful – simply by taking a few more CHANCES

At any second of our lives, new events or adventures may be just around the corner.

Right now, the phone maybe about to ring telling you that you have won £1 million on the premium bonds. Tomorrow you may have a chance meeting with a stranger who will become a significant person in your life. Or an idea may come to you as you walk down your street that will change the course of your life.

Such is the nature of chance. And it can happen at any time. But it is more likely to happen if we take actions to invite and incite it.

If we go about our lives with a sense of adventure and energy we are far more likely to have things happen in our lives than if we are sitting at home watching the telly or going about life with our eyes averted and hearts clammed shut.

In order to get the powerful force of chance and serendipity blowing more energy and events into your life, try out some of the actions below and see what happens…

- Write a letter to somebody in an old address book that you haven't spoken to in ages. Or simply phone them instead.
- Get your hair cut in a different style. (As we normally only do this at a point where we're going through a change in our lives, you can hurry up the process by getting your hair cut first.)
- Invite a crowd of people around to your home for a party.
- Listen to a radio station that you wouldn't normally listen to and follow up on something that you hear.
- Tell somebody something important that you've held back from them for years.
- Go to a library and take out a random book, a completely different

kind of book than you would normally think of.

- Move the furniture around in one of your rooms.
- Have a day where you talk to random strangers.
- Go out wearing really daring clothing and notice how people look at you differently. Enjoy acting as a different person.
- Join an evening course just for the fun of it.
- Put a pin in a map and take a trip to the place you've selected. Alternatively, just walk out of your home and get on the first bus that you see.
- Start off your day one Thursday with a luxury treat breakfast.
- Do something unexpected. Do something really daring.
- Buy something for 50p and make it your lucky charm or amulet. Make a wish on it then work towards making it come true.
- Invite a new acquaintance round for dinner, out for a drink, or a sightseeing trip perhaps.
- Volunteer your services to a voluntary organisation.
- Join a chat room or interest or support group on the internet.
- Take up a new sport or hobby or join a local group in the community.
- Wear odd shoes for the day.
- Spend a whole day just sitting in a cafe, reading and thinking.

Look for open doors. Feel the fear. But walk through them anyway.

Eureka No. 9

The No.1 secret to getting almost anything you want out of life?

Asking for it!

But you need to have a definite idea about what it is you want first…

The secret you're about to read can be used to get almost anything that you want in life – whether it's the best table at the restaurant, more time to yourself or a pay rise from your boss.

It isn't anything mystical. It isn't even that special. But if you always keep this secret in mind it can change your life dramatically.

The secret is simply that you just need to *ask* for what you're craving, lacking, or simply wanting to get your hands on.

Because the truth is that so many of us will sit around wanting or needing something without actually taking the step to ask anyone for it. If we only plucked up the courage to ask, we could so often get exactly what we are craving.

To use an example that appeared in a popular TV programme recently, Leah Newman – the wife of ex-football player Neil 'Razor' Ruddock – realised the power of this secret while appearing on *Celebrity Wife Swap*. While spending two weeks with the partner of pop star Pete Burns, she realised that there were a few extra things she wanted from her husband and her life: a bit more romance, a bit more appreciation for all she did, a bit more 'me time', and the chance to do just a few days of her old job again.

The problem had been that although she had felt all these desires, it was only when she named them that she realised these were things that she wanted – and yes, she could ask for them.

So, next time you get any kind of niggling feeling of *want* or desire, follow these 3 simple steps:

1. **Check out the feeling of want so that, in your mind, it is clear and crystalised** exactly what it is you're after.

2. **Have a really good think about what or who you can ask in order to get what you want.**

3. **Take the leap to actually ASK for it.** You may be pleasantly surprised when the person says 'yes'.

Why are we all so frightened of asking for what we want? Is it fear of hearing 'no'? Is it the playground or parental chant of "Those who ask don't get"? Are we still acting like shy children, afraid to approach the 'adults' around us? Or are we failing to recognise that other people *are* on our side in life and want to do nice things for us?

Whatever the reason, remember this:

Whenever there is something that we WANT, we may only be a tiny distance away from getting what we want (or the solution to it). Yet we will only get it if we actually make the leap to ASK for it.

Going through the motions of asking can even make you realise what you already have

Another thing you will discover about this secret is that it can actually help you realise that you *already have* some of the things that form part of your ongoing, deep-seated wants.

Suppose, for example, that you feel you have a deep desire to be and or be seen as a kind, interesting person. Chances are that you might just realise you already have this.

Or suppose, perhaps, that you are forever wishing you could be a better mother, spouse, doctor or computer programmer. There's a good chance that the very fact you're so concerned about your performance already means you're actually pretty good.

Eureka No. 10

Life too boring and predictable? Need to add a new twist of spice and adventure?

Throw a dice to give your life a completely new direction

Simply take a dice in your hand and prepare to add a new twist of chance to your life.

Dice, according to Plato, were invented by an Egyptian deity, back in the days when people believed there were external forces outside of us that determined our fate.

Today, of course, every next second – every next hour, every next day – it is we who are in total control of what will happen in our lives. We have so much choice, so much freedom. We make the rules for our own life's "game of chance".

Funnily enough, however, many of us still act as if we were not really in charge of our own life – but rather cruise along with it wherever it takes us.

In the cult seventies book, *The Dice Man*, by Luke Rhinehart, a bored psychiatrist decides to change his life of dull order and routine by using a dice to make decisions for him. Inspired by having to invent six new options for every decision he makes, his life begins to become more and more crazy – ending in him seducing the neighbor, hitting his boss, leaving his family and eventually the country…

While you might not, of course, want to take it that far, playing the dice game IS a fun way to add a little spice to your life… take a few risks… and maybe even change your fortunes entirely.

First of all you need to dig out a dice (or 'die' if we want to be correct) from the bottom of your drawers or game boxes. If you haven't got one, why not go on a shopping hunt to find one? Who knows, perhaps this act alone will take your life down a new pathway?

Next, hold it in your hand and decide what you're going to do with it.

A dice can be used to help you make a decision, help you find solutions, or simply get out of a rut and find new meals to enjoy at lunch time.

GAME NO. 1: Getting back a bit of your youthful self. First of all, think back to a time when you were really glowing with yourself and with life. Full of energy. Walking really upright and embracing every minute of life.

Now, think of six things that you used to do in those days that you don't do today and give each different choice a number from 1 to 6. (If you only want to work with three different chances, then give each choice two numbers, E.g. 1 or 2, I will play tennis... 3 or 4, I will wear perfume or aftershave... 5 or 6 I will flirt just a tiny bit with my colleagues.) Then simply throw the dice to decide which of the activities you're going to try out for the day.

When I did this myself, I ended up getting my old bike out of the shed, pumping up the tyres and enjoying a wonderful bike ride up to the common and back!

GAME NO. 2: Use it to solve a dilemma or make a difficult move in your life. Okay, suppose you're stuck in a bit of a situation at work, are worried about your daughter, or can't decide whether to blow money on a new coat for winter.

Well this time, instead of relying on your normal decision-making processes (which may err on the side of avoidance, indecision or over-caution), why not put your life in the hands of a different, more dynamic game of fortune instead?

All you have to do is think of six different actions you could take, then throw the dice to decide which you're going to go for!

GAME NO. 3: Use it to add some fun and adventure to your week. The traditional 'Dice Man' game of dice is all about using the dice to decide what you're going to do with your day. You could use it, for example, to decide what you're going to do for lunch (beans on toast 1, get the train to London and eat a hot dog in Trafalgar Square 2, make tempura 3, have tinned spaghetti 4, etc...), how you're going to spend the evening (clear out a cupboard 1, look through old photos 2, write a letter to an old friend 3, eat dinner in bed 4, take a walk 5, write a poem or song 6) or which of the people at work you're going to choose to say something nice to today…

Have a go! I promise you it will be fun!

Eureka No. 11

Your happiness and success in life may be blocked by expectations that are either too high or too low

This one-minute exercise may change the rest of your life...

The hopes, dreams and expectations we have of ourselves and our lives have a strong and direct impact on how happy and satisfied we feel – and on what we actually achieve.

If our expectations are too high then we may never feel satisfied. If our expectations of satisfaction or achievement or happiness are too low then we may be damning our life before it even gets started.

The exercise below is borrowed from the psychologist Dorothy Rowe and just might change the rest of your life:

First of all, take a piece of paper and write down an answer to this question:

"How old will you be when you die?"

Next, bearing that age in mind, think about and answer the four questions below, one question at a time:

- Why did you choose that age?
- What do you *hope* to do between now and then?
- What do you expect you will do between now and then?
- Why are there differences between what you hope and expect, and what can you do to overcome these differences?

Might you, for example, want to tone down the things you hope for and realise that you can become more satisfied with what you already have or are likely to achieve? Or is it more the case, perhaps, that you hope for too little? Or expect too little from yourself?

Some serious soul searching may be in order!

Eureka No. 12

One of life's great procrastinators? Here's what your delaying habits can tell you about your psychology, your beliefs or your fear of success...

Do you put off dealing with the big things or just annoying mundane jobs? Is your procrastination just a practical issue? Or does it restrict and suffocate the whole of your life?

Whichever of the many forms of procrastination you suffer from, recognising and getting on top of it can make an enormous impact in improving your life. It can also teach you some interesting things about you as a person.

While it is in no way exhaustive, the list of causes and solutions below can go a long way towards helping you pinpoint your own kind of procrastination and working towards fixing it. The important thing to remember is that whatever kind of procrastination you're suffering from, it IS solvable.

1. It could just be a simple case of finding the task unpleasant...

First of all there is what the psychologists call simple 'task-related procrastination'. This could include not wanting to do the washing up, for example, never getting round to switching your telephone provider, or disliking certain elements of your work which you feel are too mundane, meaningless or boring.

One solution to this kind of procrastination is to try and give yourself daily reminders of the positive consequences of performing these tasks. Another is to actually give yourself little rewards for pushing yourself to do the jobs you quite simply don't want to do. It is often the lack of perceived reward in a job that stops us from wanting to do it, so offering ourselves a reward can be a surprisingly simple but effective solution.

2. Is there a psychological reason behind your dislike of this particular task?

Also looking at specific task-related procrastination, there is another simple question you might need to ask yourself: Are there any psychological reasons why I just never seem to want to get down to this particular kind of task? You might realise, for example, that you are simply rebelling against a task that a parent made you do as a child which you resented. Or it could help you highlight an area of your life where you have a particular problem.

3. Is your procrastination caused by your personality traits or beliefs about what life should be like?

We all have some general, deep-seated beliefs about life that inform the way we believe things should be, and these can often sit at the bottom of our personal habits of procrastination. While these beliefs can sometimes have some very positive sides to them, they can also prevent us from wanting to get down to things.

Here are a few of those beliefs:

Do any of these character types sound like you?

- Some people, for example, have the belief that life should always be easy and pleasant so they actually have an enormous problem getting down to jobs that are difficult.
- Other people have acquired the belief that they are not very clever, talented or lucky. Perhaps this was something they were told as a child or have been made to feel as an adult. Either way, this kind of belief will certainly stop you from even trying to do things if you believe you are not good enough to be able to do them, nor fortunate enough in life to gain this advantage or achievement.
- Perfectionism is another 'condition' that affects some people and can even border on the obsessive compulsive. While most of us realise that nobody in life actually gets anywhere near achieving perfection

in anything, there are some who believe that perfection is not only possible but necessary. It's very hard to start any project if you're haunted by this kind of belief. See Eureka No. 13 (The secret of success is the ability to fail) for further inspiration.

- Another kind of belief that can put serious dampeners on all areas of your life is the desire for certainty, the desire to play it safe. You'll know this if you feel the need to ask dozens of questions about a task or enterprise before you're prepared to even engage with it – and then you still feel nervous about what will happen or what's expected of you. But you'll spend your whole life preparing for life instead of just taking a plunge at it if you don't confront this tendency.

4. The key to your procrastination could lie in your childhood and be the key to your whole life

"Regardless of our level of procrastination," says psychologist Karen E. Peterson in her book *The Tomorrow Trap*, "it's much easier to be ashamed about being late than it is to feel ashamed about finishing the task or making the decision, only to be told we've performed poorly. In this way, procrastination actually protects us from tapping into this pool of deeper feelings we'd just as soon avoid."

On one level I think we can all be guilty of this to an extent. If I throw myself into a task with complete gusto and devote as much time to it as it needs, for example, then I won't have any excuse for the imperfection of my achievement.

On another level, however, Ms. Peterson believes that the cause of this kind of procrastination is a deep feeling of shame that many of us carry within us. It prevents us from living a full and happy life. "We must learn," she says, "how to conquer this lack of motivation in order to avoid a diminished sense of spirituality in our lives".

When you think you're worthless

The answer, says Peterson, is to explore our procrastination in order to uncover the sources of our own personal inner 'shame', ' unloveableness' or plain lack of self confidence. Only when we have realised what these sources are can we actually take charge of our lives, live without shame, and stop living in fear of others.

Factors and events that can be identified as childhood triggers for shame include:

- Perceived or real physical imperfections – such as having to wear glasses or feeling unhappy with your body.
- Disruptions in normal parenting – which includes parents not being able to give you full attention as an infant because of such things as their own personal problems or the arrival of a second child.
- Neglect or childhood abuse.
- Flaws in normal parenting – for example, being called the black sheep of the family or growing up in a family that believed the world was against them.

Only by understanding the source of our shame or unloveableness as a child can we decide to move beyond it as an adult.

"Procrastination" said the poet Edward Young, "is the thief of time."

I also believe it can be the thief of a better life.

Eureka No. 13

The secret of success is the ability to fail

This is true of everything from playing rounders and cake-making through to success in relationships and your work. The less risks you're prepared to take, the smaller will be your gains.

If you're not prepared for the fact that your efforts may end in a minor temporary failure, then you won't put enough effort in to succeed.

Whenever we try hard to achieve something, we are also putting our trust in hope – and when hope is involved, so in uncertainty.

The key, perhaps, is to take a lighter attitude towards failure, a lighter attitude towards ourselves. Have a readiness to laugh and ask others to laugh with us.

As Robert Browning once said,

"A minute's success pays the failure of years."

Or, in the words of Sir Winston Churchill, a man with a tremendous ability for both sublime failure and success:

"Success is the ability to go from one failure to another with no loss of enthusiasm."

Eureka! No. 14

Eureka No. 14

Need to make a difficult decision?

It's not so much what you decide that counts, but what you DO with that decision

Many people are paralysed by decisions because they are frightened that the option they choose may be the wrong one – or worse than what they already have.

What this often means is that they stick with what they are more familiar with, instead of making a brave move to something different.

The problem with comfort zones, however, is that they are often not that comfortable. Sure, there may be some feeling of safety about them, but they're normally also accompanied by a selection of other emotions including feeling that you're stuck in a rut or feeling trapped... boredom... discontent... feelings of inadequacy... unhappiness... or a worry that you will get to the end of your life and wish that you had lived it better.

So what if you took the attitude that it doesn't so much matter which of the options you choose but rather what you make of that decision? The wrong attitude in the first place can make every option a disaster. The right attitude can turn whichever option you choose into a life-affirming experience.

For starters, if you're having trouble making a decision or deciding what you're going to do with your life, take some consolation in the fact that it goes with the territory. And what wonderful territory it is to be human.

If you are feeling the pain of having to decide whether to stay or leave a partner, is this not because on the plus side you have or will also experience in your life the immense joy of human love? If you are having trouble making a decision about your career, is it not partly because, as human beings, we can appreciate the satisfaction of doing a job or an activity where – even though perhaps only sporadically or fleetingly – we feel like we're on top of the world, doing what we do, being who we are as a unique and talented individual?

Yes, it is true that as human beings we are acutely aware that one day we will die, our time will come, and we will look back and lament if we have spent our lives in the wrong job or with the wrong miserable partner (as opposed to the right miserable one?). But isn't it that same fear, that existential angst about getting it right, which also allows us to live our lives with the intensity and search for meaning that makes life so full of awe, glory and occasionally heart-bursting happiness?

The TRUTH about making decisions

That is not to say, of course, that all our mental strife will help us make the right decision. As Harvard Professor of Psychology Daniel Gilbert says in his book *Stumbling on Happiness*, we – our present selves – are constantly trying to do the right thing for our future selves, so that they will be able to feel happy, fulfilled, thin and healthy… become immune from money worries… or have enough money when they're older to buy houses for each of the children, go on four holidays every year and *finally* have the entire house beautifully and perfectly redecorated.

Yet, as Professor Gilbert says, even the very best thought-out decisions made today may not turn out to be what our future selves desire:

"Like the fruits of our loins, our temporary progeny are often thankless. We toil and sweat to give them just what we think they will like, and they quit their jobs, grow their hair, move to or from San Fransisco and wonder how we could ever have been stupid enough to think they'd like that.

"We fail to achieve the accolades and rewards that we consider crucial to their well-being, and they end up thanking God that things didn't work out according to out shortsighted, misguided plan. Even that person who takes a bite of the cupcake we purchased a few minutes earlier may make a sour face and accuse us of having bought the wrong snack."

So what if you're still worried about making the wrong decision?

Even if you do get it wrong you've got a really good defence: You didn't have a crystal ball. You were unable to look into the future. You made the best decision you could given the information available to you.

You don't know what you will want later – or what will be the right thing for you next year. You only know what you want now and what you feel is the right thing for you *now*. You can't predict. You can only try.

Remember, it is not always so much what you decide that counts as much as what you make of that decision.

Part of making the most of a decision includes knowing when to accept that what you chose was WRONG and reversing that decision rather than stubbornly or lazily sticking with it.

In his book, *What Should I Do With my Life?*, author Po Bronson tells the stories of hundreds of people who have done incredible things to change and redirect their lives. An important point he is very keen to make, however, is that the decisions these people made never jumped out at them as the obvious choice to make.

> *"Do not wait for the kind of clarity that comes with epiphanies. In the nine hundred plus stories I heard in my research, almost nobody was struck with an epiphany… Don't doubt your desire because it comes to you as a whisper; don't think, 'If it were really important to me, I'd feel clearer about this, less conflicted.' My research didn't show that to be true. The things we really want to do are usually the ones that scare us the most. The things you'll not feel conflicted about are the choices that leave no one hurt."*

Your Happiness and Satisfaction

Eureka No.15

How to transport yourself from the mundane negativity of life to sheer bliss at any moment

Instead of adapting the pathological human tendency to dwell on the negative, you can choose to embrace the sheer beauty and awesomeness of life every day.

How? Most of us will happily waste half our day worrying about a tiny mistake we've made or a spot on our chin – yet few of us will spare even two minutes to stare in wonder at the mind-blowing reality of the stars, or the hundreds of microscopic miracles at work within our fingers.

When we are fretting about something or dwelling on the negative, chances are we are living in a world of ideas and images inside our head. Our point of focus becomes what is going on inside of our thoughts, instead of what is going on around us, and our energy will be concentrated in our minds rather than our bodies. A simple antidote to this, therefore, is to move our attention to the REAL world around us – to the physical rather than the mental, the true rather than the imagined.

Pick something up and examine it closely. Stare at your hands. Go for a walk up a hill, and feel the enormity of it beneath your feet. Immerse yourself in the enormous world of wonders around you – rather than seeing your current mood, problem or even self as the centre of the universe. Focus your attention on the outside, not the in.

Eureka No.16

You can dramatically improve the self image you have of yourself by investigating where you got it from

There is a lot of talk about whether or not we have 'confidence' or even 'self confidence'. It has become such a popular term, in fact, that it is now a catch-all term for any kind of social anxiety, shyness or low self esteem we might suffer – and there almost seems to be a dividing line between the haves and the have nots.

But perhaps more important and fundamental than this 'confidence' thing is the self *image* that we have of ourselves.

You have no doubt come across or met people who have a far higher opinion of themselves and their attributes than you feel are justified. And then there are other people who have a very poor self image that is at odds with reality. You will even meet people who believe they are tall when they are not… thin people who think they're fat… and dumb as you like bigheads who think they're Mensa material.

Every single one of us would benefit from exploring the opinions we currently have of ourselves and taking a closer look at whether or not they're justified, and where these opinions might have come from. Often the source is quite obvious to unearth, but it can help us to immediately reassess and change any faulty opinion we might have if we recognise the source. It is also important to remember that many of the opinions we hold about ourselves may have been formed when we were much younger, and there is a very good chance we might have changed a lot since then.

Take a few minutes to write a description of yourself for each of the categories opposite according to your current opinions about yourself. Next, spend time thinking about where and when – and how – each of the opinions were formed, and what you can do to change those opinions when you realise they are too exaggerated, too negative, too damaging or just plain wrong in any way.

Do be prepared, however, for some resistance in changing these opinions of yourself. Not only have we become accustomed to seeing ourselves in this way, but in many cases we have come to use our weaknesses or attributes as a kind of excuse for our life. Not being able to blame our fate or bad luck any longer can put a lot more responsibility on ourselves for being in charge of our own lives.

Your Height –

Your Body –

Your Looks –

Your Intelligence –

Your Talent –

Your Ambition –

Your Likelihood of Success –

Your Spirituality –

Your Outlook –

Your Aptitude for Happiness –

Your Confidence –

Your Abilities –

Eureka No. 17

The beliefs we have about ourselves and about life can condemn us to unhappiness, stress, under-achievement and depression

But if we change the things we believe to be true in life, we can even change how life IS...

Do you believe that money is something you should be careful with and that spending too much is sinful? Or are you of the opinion that money is there for spending?

Do you believe that life is generally wonderful? Or that life is basically terrible?

Do you believe that you are a fundamentally good person? Or a fundamentally bad one?

Do you believe that you should work really hard? Or do you believe that you should do as little work as you can get away with?

None of these beliefs about life are of course right or wrong. But whichever view we take can have an enormous impact on our life. Being able to soften the views that we have can enable us to cut ourselves some slack, see things a little differently, or resist a certain behavior or habit of thought that is creating a barrier to our happiness.

You see, the truth about life, the universe, meaning, happiness and human knowledge is that the world and life are not so much how they are but HOW YOU SEE THEM instead. The views that you have about life are therefore crucial to whether you are rich, successful, satisfied or dissatisfied. Your view can even be instrumental in whether you enjoy your children, respect your wife or like drinking coffee.

Take, for example, the fundamental belief that some people have that life should be easy (perhaps picked up from having life made easy for them as a child and teenager?). For people with this view of life, they will always have trouble dealing with any kind of discomfort, hard work or difficulty. For someone who has the opposite view, however, the view that life is always hard work and miserable can become a self-fulfilling prophecy.

Views that we have, of course, are not always general ones about life, but may be more specific to our own life – or be rules that we have for ourselves but do not expect others to live by. Just a few examples of the kinds of beliefs that can sometimes be harmful, destructive or unhelpful (as well as in some ways useful, of course) include:

- I should do everything I do perfectly.
- If I am having fun I am wasting my time.
- I do not have enough time to do what I want.
- The way I do things is the best way.
- Men only want looks in a woman.
- Women are only after your money.
- My husband doesn't care about me.
- My wife just takes but gives very little.
- All I want to do in life is become a professional cyclist and nothing else will make me happy.

Another thing that can happen is that beliefs that we formed about certain parts of our life in the past may no longer be true. Yet we carry on believing them.

I remember clearly, for example, the day I realised that the opinion I had of myself as a shy, background, half-invisible person needed updating. While this opinion may have been justified at the age of 13, it was no longer justified or useful for a 30-year old woman in charge of a large, busy department in a successful publishing company. More recently I have realised that the view I had of how difficult my life was with two small children needs softening and updating. Now that they have reached an age where they're easier, I can allow myself to admit how much joy they bring to my life and how much I adore them.

In fact, I need to remind myself on a regular basis that life is not – as my mother told me one day when I objected to doing the hoovering – "all about having to do things we don't want to do." It was a subtle but transforming change I made to my life (and indeed myself) when I realised that my attitude to all my chores (childcare, washing up, cooking, working) could became one of thanks and pleasure, instead of a feeling of heavy reluctance and a belief that life should never be fun but always damned hard work.

While some beliefs or views about life can have a relatively mild negative influence on our happiness and satisfaction, some of them can go as far as to make us clinically depressed or even psychotic. Psychotherapist Dorothy Rowe has identified a list of six absolute, unquestionable truths that she has found depressed patients seem to have about their lives:

- No matter how good and nice I appear to be, I am really bad, evil, valueless, unacceptable to myself and other people.
- Other people are such that I must fear, hate and envy them.
- Life is terrible and death is worse.
- Only bad things happened to me in the past and only bad things will happen to me in the future.
- It is wrong to get angry.
- I must never forgive anyone, least of all myself.

(Taken from *Depression: The Way Out of Your Prison* by Dorothy Rowe)

Beliefs like these will damage if not destroy your life. By realising that you can switch off, soften or change them, it is perfectly possible to rewrite the blueprint of your life – and especially your future. By changing the message (or by reprogamming the software if you like), you can switch your entire life and mind onto a brand new track. For some, this realisation in itself is enough to make a change happen instantly. For others, it will take some more serious dedication and effort to overcome so many years of negative self opinions.

Eureka No.18

You CAN live life on the high wire yet feel calm and unflustered

Cope with life better by creating yourself a confidence-giving safety net

Why do so many of life's little tasks and tribulations fill our whole lives with so much dread and horror?

Why do you *still* feel nervous about walking into a social or business gathering or speaking in front of people?

Why can something like having to make a phone call about a parking ticket put a shadow over your whole day and constrict your heart until it feels like concrete?

Part of it, of course, has to do with... OTHER PEOPLE – you know, that alien species that may look just like you but are in fact evil monsters who will eat us if we talk to them. Part of it has to do with our human habit of blowing things out of proportion and always latching onto whatever is negative or threatening. And another part is simply a question of *confidence*.

To be confident in the way that such situations demand does not need you to think you are a perfect, amazing person. What is required instead is that you rationally accept that you are capable of the task, and at least equal to those around you, with charms and skills of your own.

All that most tasks require, in take, is sufficient confidence in your ability to carry them out – and a healthy acceptance of the possibility and perfect acceptability of imperfection or even failure. Which is what we call the 'safety net'.

Adapted from an idea from executive coach Neil Fiore, the safety net is an idea that can enable you to complete a task without postponing or procrastinating out of fear of failure – or subjecting your poor ego to self-inflicted psychological torture in the process.

Imagine, Neil says, that the task you need to achieve is like having to walk along a plank that is one foot wide and 30 feet long, lying on the ground. Now, this is probably what the difficulty of the task is in reality. But there's a chance that, in your mind, the plank looks more like it's balanced between the top of two high New York buildings, with a 1000-foot drop underneath.

Now here's the secret: All you have to do is imagine that there's a safety net underneath you. The safety net may be your self esteem in general which you can bolster before you start. Remind yourself of all your charms and qualities and the things you are good at. Say complimentary things about yourself in your head. And reassure yourself that all of us are imperfect and other people would make mistakes in this situation too.

Alternatively, you can create a safety net by using a simple and well-thought out rational statement to sooth and counteract your panicking. If you have a friend coming round for dinner, for example, and are panicking about the meal being bad, ask yourself what's the worse that could happen and how bad that could be.

The main idea is that whenever you panic over a task you need to perform, reassure yourself that it won't be a problem – even if you fall…

Ongoing stress causes us to make mountains out of molehills and live our lives as if the sky were falling down

Another thing worth bearing in mind is that many of us tend to worry disproportionately about the smallest concerns. If we are the kind of person who lives in a state of constant stress, our minds are obliged to be constantly and neurotically on the look out for the negative. As you've no doubt been told before, stress is the state we need to be in if we're out hunting for bears or tigers, or if feel that we are about to be captured by the enemy. It's useful in such a state to expect a crocodile to be hidden behind the filing cabinet – or for a man in army uniform to publicly humiliate you and strip you of your job, your home and your children if you fumble your words slightly on the telephone. But it's not a very useful way to go about your day.

This stress phenomenon is in fact where sufferers of both anxiety and depression start and never finish. Because you're stressed, you'll find other things to be stressed about. The adrenalin your body's pumping makes your mind see a mountain where there's a molehill.

Understanding what is at play is a good place to start in conquering this problem. Try asking yourself to place the current problem or situation on a scale where 'No Problem' is at one end and 'Life Threatening' is at the other. Once you've downsized the severity of the problem in your mind, create yourself a safety net to survive it. Then take wing and fly over it!

Eureka No. 19

Why are we all suffering from Delight Deficiency Syndrome?

Sometimes we can get so bogged down with hard work, anxiety, problems and exhaustion that we fall into a state of being where we're heads down, drudging through life and failing to smell the roses or notice the beauty of the moon.

There is a sparsity of fun, a sparsity of colour, and certainly no room for smiling or laughter. Rather than living joyously and lightly in the beauty of the present, we obsess about all the negatives in our lives until we're buried under a blanket of gloom.

The most crucial step in getting out of this dreary situation is recognising we're in it – and we're almost always suffering from at least some degree of it at most times of our life. Next, try whatever ideas you can think of to start acting more like a dog having fun in the park than it's woe-laden owner. Go out of your way to add more pleasure, delight and brightness to your life.

- Laugh at how seriously you are taking everything. As Voltaire said, "God is a comedian playing to an audience too afraid to laugh."
- Do something creative that's just for you – whether it's a cartoon of your boss, a poem about a man who loved string, or a painting of a row of belly buttons.
- Play music really loud and dance and sing along to it.
- Take the kids to a funfair – or up the hill to fly a kite. I remember, in fact, taking my daughter to a park recently and noticing her shout "wheee" every time the swing swung forward. "I need more 'wheee' in my life" was the thought that occurred to me!
- Put by a weekend where you're going to do nothing but have fun.
- Sit in a bath with too many bubbles in it – reading a joke book.
- Do something really silly, frivolous or even downright immature.

- Go out and have some FUN, pleasure or *delight* RIGHT NOW.
- Write a long list of all the positive things in your life and carry it around with you.
- Spend time looking after and pampering that 'you' who puts themselves under all this pressure.

And don't forget to bring more fun and pleasure to your workplace as well. People generally work better, faster and more creatively when they're in a more positive and happy mood. ***Spending every minute of the day working may make you feel that you're trying your hardest and not slacking, but it may actually be making you less productive.*** The work environment of many offices and work places could also do with an injection of fun into them. In fact, I challenge any business to add something like a football table or the latest video game and discover that it doesn't *increase* productivity.

In an article she wrote just before she died, founder of the Body Shop Anita Roddick asks us to imagine that the government has decided that Beauty should form a central part of its manifesto and that it has made her a minister responsible for public spaces.

"The first thing I would discover once I was behind my Whitehall desk," she says "would be that the job wouldn't just be fun: it would be really inexpensive. The first thing I would do is organise a day of Common Delight, an annual carnival of beauty which could turn the world upside down. The second item on the agenda would be to draft a new law for billboards. They would no longer be allowed to sell products; only poetry and art would be allowed."

Turn activist to embrace life

Clinical psychologist and author of *Commonsense Rebellion*, Bruce E. Levine, says that "one of the best long-term antidotes to depression is some form of social activism. The world today, especially in the West, seems to contain many demoralised and dispirited individuals who doubt their capacity to change the world for the better… Local activism can also give people a greater sense of autonomy and a belief that what they say and what they care about actually has some political impact. This feeling, in turn, can be a source of energy and improved morale that can act as a lifelong, and sustainable, antidote to depression."

And finally, also bear in mind that while you may feel selfish asking for time to enjoy yourself when things like your work and your kids already need every second, don't forget that they too will suffer if we're overburdening ourselves and becoming moody because of it. Enjoying yourself will increase the amount of happiness you can give to others – as well as the creativity and energy you can give to work.

Eureka No. 20

How the Taoist art of "effortless doing" can allow you to live life more calmly, productively and with more spiritual fulfillment

Sometimes our lives can seem so busy, so full of urgent tasks, that it feels like the effort we put in is much greater than the results we get out.

Barely have we finished washing up the plates on a Sunday evening than it's time to get back onto the Monday morning treadmill. And nowhere in the week have you had the time to sort your head out, stare out of a window, or ring the builders!

You're aware that there are things going on in that head up there but you simply haven't had the chance to slow down and listen to what those quiet little voices are mumbling, worrying or crying about. You're also aware that there must be better ways of going about your life – if only you had time to slow down and think about it.

If you feel that you're forever tackling your life like a captain of a ship trying to survive a raging typhoon (and you may also have the tension headaches or furrowed brow to prove it), then come back for regular visits to this page and a dose of this therapeutic teaching from Taoism.

In this ancient Chinese philosophy, 'wu-wei' is the art of effortless doing, of acting through not acting. Nature, the teaching tells us, doesn't need to make a huge *conscious* shoulder-clenching brain effort to make the first early blossom flowers appear on the dark forsaken wood of the twigs of the trees. A river doesn't stress about the correct course of its flow around each corner. These are things that just happen.

Life just flows. And if we can take a leaf out of nature's book, we too can float more effortlessly through our own lives with the delicacy, beauty and simplicity of a cherry blossom.

Rather than subjecting ourselves to too much stress by making too much effort in life, we can take more of a back seat. **Allow life to take its own course and become more of an observer.** Because life will happen anyway. Just as Tao makes the sun rise it will make you move your arm. And the more we resist and fight it the more painful and less enjoyable it will be.

Indeed, it is often when we act with **inner stillness** and quiet activity that we not only appreciate the fine artistic display which is the flow of life, but enjoy more success in it as well.

Remember too the power of doing nothing. In the famous book, *The Tao of Pooh*, Benjamin Hoff tells us how Pooh is the one who finds Eyore's missing tail. While all the other busy animals rush around searching for it, Pooh notices it simply by sitting around doing nothing.

This is not to say, of course, that you can simply sit in an armchair all day and the hoover will silently tidy and clean the house, then put itself away again. But rather, instead of fretting about what will happen next and moving hectically towards doing it, **find a place of inner quiet and watch thoughtfully as the activity begins to flow.**

Try it at work. Try it at home. Try it in social situations when you feel anxious about what to do. Press play and wait for the magic of life to unfold. Smile as you watch it happen. Breathe deeply and slowly as you start effortlessly to act. Do everything you do with calm purpose, and you will have a more productive day than if you run about like you were in a supermarket grab.

Be more receptive than pro-active and great things may happen, too. Above all, try not to worry too much about tomorrow, but rather rejoice in watching what happens to you today. The future will happen without our having to make stressful efforts to plan for it.

Eureka No. 21

Exorcise the ghosts of grievances past and the hurts you have suffered at the hands of others

The treatment we have had at the hands of others can stay with us and affect us for life. There is a lot we can do, however, to reduce that pain of those wounds.

Exorcise your grievances and decide not to allow these events to create a shadow over your life or continue to mar you today.

Why continue suffering when you have suffered once already? Why allow this single person to carry on affecting your life? What is stopping you from *letting go*?

One of the most powerful techniques you can use to heal and exorcise these hurts and disarm this person's power over your life is to write a long letter to the person involved. This could be A Letter of Goodbye, A Letter of Clearance, A Letter of Forgiveness, or A Letter to Hear Me Out.

Set a time one day or evening where you will have at least an hour or so of uninterrupted peaceful time to carry out this life-transforming, burden-lightening exercise.

You do not need to think hard about what to say as much as just let the words flow from deep within you and appear on the paper. Connect back to the past, but express it in the present. And then clear a new brighter path for your future.

Start your letter with their name, writing Dear…

Then see what happens next. You might want to say, perhaps, "When you did what you did to me…" or "I just want you to know…" or "How could you possibly…?"

This outlet alone may be enough to get an enormous weight off your chest. It may also offer some important insights into who you are and why you feel like you do.

What it is important to remember, however, is that if you realise how these experiences have affected the way you behave or think, then making that realisation could be the key you need to free you from those behaviours or thoughts. You do not have to accept them forever, but can choose to move on from them and live your life how you wish.

A further step in this process might be to write a letter back to you from the person you have written to. Perhaps they will say sorry to you. Perhaps they will try to explain to you what lead them to do what they did – and this may allow you some insight of understanding and healing. It is very rare that the other person has really wanted us to feel the pain that we did.

Eureka No. 22

Stop 'catastrophising' about your life and calling yourself bad names

Banish negative words from your mind and notice an increase in happiness and self worth IMMEDIATELY

Single words can be incredibly powerful and can have an enormous effect on the human mind. It is likely, for example, that you are not even aware of some of the destructive vocabulary that you might use on yourself. It may be such a background voice in your head that you don't even realise you're calling yourself a loser, an idiot, stupid or unlovable. Yet if you repeat words like these often enough you will come to believe them.

Another place where the wrong word can be destructive is when you're anticipating an event or something you need to do. Having to make a phone call may be labeled 'awful', for example, or the meeting you have this week may already be labeled 'terrible' in your mind.

The secret of this Eureka is to pay attention to what you're saying to yourself in the back of your mind whenever you're feeling down or uncomfortable. Then, when you've spotted the destructive thoughts, make moves to correct them.

Instead of muttering "I'm such an idiot for missing that deadline," for example, try saying: "Missing that deadline was a really bad move. I'm really disappointed about it..."

Instead of thinking "Oh no, making that phone call is going to be horrible," try saying "I seem to feel a bit worried about making that phone call, but like all these things, it will be over quickly and it's never as bad as I think."

Don't let your thoughts run away with you and create feelings you don't want to feel

The key to remember is that the thoughts you think make you feel how you feel. Whenever you realise that you are feeling bad or unhappy, listen in to the thoughts that are going on in your head. Are those thoughts appropriate? Could they be kinder? Are you judging yourself too harshly or giving yourself a harder time than you need to?

Then consciously replace those words with some new key sentences or thoughts for the situation.

Our thoughts can sometimes act like a very harsh commentator on our lives. But it's *your* head, remember, so *you* can decide what it is that the voice says!

Practice a comforting internal voice

If you're feeling a bit down, check out not just what the voices in your head are saying to you, but also *the tone of voice* they're talking in as well. Chances are you may be saying really quite horrible things to yourself that are making you feel bad – such as "Nobody will ever really love you…You are fat and stupid….My life is so terrible."

If you find yourself saying negative things to yourself in your head (and often there's a voice or two up there that can be really spiteful and mean to you), try developing a comforting and warm voice that says nicer things to you instead. You don't, of course, have to go over the top with niceness. But I bet you can make the voice a lot nicer and more realistic than the one that's currently shooting your confidence to pieces. It may help to write down some positive messages to yourself that you can refer to when you need them.

Eureka No. 23

Pass by your adversities as if they were mountains and you were calmly walking down a valley

When adversity happens in our life, it is often our wont to throw ourselves onto the tracks in front of it. It consumes us. It becomes us. It flows through our veins and hearts instead of life. Every bit of our energy is eaten up with trying to deal with it.

But what if we were able to step aside from our troubles and be a bit more of an observer, as well? Perhaps you might picture yourself sat up on a quiet hill while the adversity passes by below like a steam train on its tracks. Perhaps you'd rather see the adversity as a mountain and yourself as a hiker walking past it in the valley. Or perhaps you could find yourself in a retreat somewhere – a quiet room in your mind's imagination or a cottage in the woods.

By trying to resist adversity and fight against it, we only make it more painful. By accepting it and watching it, we can get some valuable distance from it.

Challenges and difficulties can often be better handled through the power of effortless activity – of acceptance first, plus thoughtful and purposeful passivity. A way will come if you sit slowly and wait – just as the mighty river has changed the shape of the landscape simply by flowing slowly and effortlessly on.

We should be flexible to change, open to the new. And great power and clarity will come to us, enabling us to be so much bigger than every challenge.

Eureka No. 24

ACT *as if* you're happy and the reality will often follow…

Climbing out of depression can take some great leaps of faith

When we're feeling depressed, we tend to stop taking part in activities that might offer us fun or enjoyment and therefore relief from our negative feelings and a shoehorn out of them. One of the main reasons for this is that when you are feeling low, it is very difficult to project yourself into any proposed situation and imagine yourself enjoying it.

The psychology of the human mind means that when you're feeling a certain feeling or sensation, it takes up all your being – and there's no room for letting in another feeling or sensation, not even an imagined one. The feeling of the moment takes up all the space.

Take how you feel after an enormous meal, for example. It's very difficult then to imagine wanting to eat again. Likewise, when you're feeling unhappy, it's very difficult to get any kind of picture of yourself feeling good. **When you're feeling down you can only imagine you will always feel like that.** Life will always be terrible, it seems, and nothing is worth bothering with.

The key here is not to wait for the desire to do things in the future to come, but rather to schedule activities now – even if you don't want to do them. Signing up for an adult learning course could be perfect, for example, as it not only gives you the stimulus of learning or creativity (what better compliment to depression than the smell of clay or the curved line of a pot?), but also much-needed social contact as well.

Other good activities are any kind of physical activity, especially walking on hills or in woods. Try ten pin bowling, drinks or lunch with a friend, gardening, getting involved in local charities or pressure groups…anything that keeps your mind off of all those negative thoughts that are making you feel depressed in the first place.

Scheduling in activity will probably feel like the last thing you can bring yourself to do. Sitting on the edge of your bed for hours, staring into space seems a far more pressing activity for you at the moment. The key here, therefore, may be to find a piece of paper (coloured if you have it) and start writing down some activities or instructions to yourself. Depending on how low and inactive you've been of late, this might start as simply as "Tomorrow: Have a really nice shower, put some nice clothes on and walk to the shops to buy a bunch of flowers and some cornflakes." Then you work up from there.

Eureka No. 25

Why do we fear death – yet moan about life so much as well?

For many of us, perhaps, a fear of death is a fear that we are not living our life particularly well or getting enough from it. Time is running out for us to find happiness, to find forgiveness, or to prove that we are somebody or achieve what we have set out to do.

And yes – to an extent, the day of our death *will* be our own personal judgment day. But rather than see this is a negative thing, we can choose to embrace the closeness of our death and use it to make us live our lives more keenly.

Ask yourself: What are the things I will wish that I'd done more of when I die? What are the things that I will wish I had done less?

More importantly, *let yourself off the hook.* If you spend your whole life trying to perform or achieve the high levels of achievement you have set for yourself, you will live your life in the shadow of the fear of not achieving them.

Let yourself off the hook and find glory in just living instead.

Can closeness to death make us live our lives better?

In his book, *The Gift of Therapy*, author and eminent psychologist, Irvin Yalom, says that in group therapy groups for cancer patients he would often find them lamenting how they only wish they had learnt to live this way before they had been struck by cancer:

"In the years I worked with terminally ill patients, I saw a great many patients who, facing death, underwent significant and positive personal change. Patients felt they had grown wise; they re-prioritized their values and began to trivialise the trivia in their lives. It was as though cancer cured neurosis – phobias and crippling interpersonal concerns seemed to melt away."

"After your death you will be what you were before your birth."
Arthur Schopenhauer

"She closed her eyes; and in sweet slumber lying,
her spirit tiptoed from its lodging place.
It's folly to shrink in fear, if this is dying;
for death looked lovely in her lovely face."
Petrarch, 14th Century Italian poet

"For what is it to die but to stand naked in the wind and to melt into the sun?
And what is to cease breathing, but to free the breath from its restless tides, that it may rise and expand and seek God unencumbered?
Only when you drink from the river of silence shall you indeed sing.
And when you have reached the mountain top, then you shall begin to climb.
And when the earth shall claim your limbs, then shall you truly dance."
Kahil Gibran, The Prophet

Eureka No. 26

Feeling a bit down, distressed, vulnerable or overwhelmed?

Ask yourself kindly what you need to feel better

You may well have been told before that you need to learn to love yourself more. As well as calling for a healthy level of self esteem and a positive self image, this is also a question of offering yourself the warmth of love when you're feeling empty or troubled inside.

Whenever you find yourself feeling particularly distressed or vulnerable, turn your attention warmly and lovingly inward towards yourself. Tune into yourself at a deeper level and ask yourself what is going on. Instead of the harsh, critical and sometimes even bullying voice with which we sometimes speak to ourselves, use loving self-talk to comfort, reassure and make yourself feel loved. Ask yourself what you need to feel better.

Sit down to do this, and allow some time for the answers to surface. Don't just be satisfied with the first few you get initially, but allow the question to sit for longer and for more answers to come.

Eureka No. 27

Drop the heaviness of your SELF and make room for more bliss and lightness

It is ironic, perhaps, that words like 'lightness' and 'bliss' make many people sneer. It is partly 21st century cynicism no doubt, but also partly due to our addiction to the *heavy*.

In the modern age we carry around with us egos the size of cargo ships – laden to sinking with guilt, worries, negativity, self-doubting, self-obsessing, hypocrisy and fear. Not to mention the last episode of Big Brother or East Enders, a shopping list for the next three day's meals and a To-Do list that it will probably take the next three years to accomplish.

But what would it be like if we were able to literally 'drop' our heavy load, in the same way as you would drop a heavy boulder if it was giving you pain to carry it…?

In his best-selling book, *The Power of Now*, Eckhart Tolle tells the story of how he awoke one night feeling miserable, loathsome and with the thought in his head "I cannot live with myself any longer." Then suddenly, he says "I became aware of what a peculiar thought it was.

"Am I one or two? If I cannot live with myself, there must be two of me: the 'I' and the 'self' that 'I' cannot live with. 'Maybe,' I thought, 'only one of them is real'…"

Tolle then proceeded to have a profound spiritual experience where he completely lost the whole of his 'self' and spent years living in a state of bliss, just marveling at the world around him.

Few of us will be lucky enough to kick the self into touch so rapidly. But how much happier would we all be if we could at the very least manage to lighten it a little?

The mind, says Eckhart Tolle, is really a tool that we use. But it has become so increasingly all-present and powerful that we have now got to the stage where we believe that we are what we think. We have come to associate with it so much, we actually believe that we *are* all that stuff going on inside the over-active machine gone mad which is our mind.

The first step in lightening ourselves and freeing ourselves from the pain of the mind and ego is to realise that we *can* disconnect ourselves from it. Try to be more the 'I' that is observing and just being rather than the 'me' that's eating itself up with anger, resentment or anxiety. **Observe the mind at work as if it was separate from you, not as if it is you.**

Whenever you can, focus on the *present* moment right now. The mind is forever thinking about the past or the future, but when you are truly *being* and living as yourself you are strongly present in the NOW. In the world around you. In your physical being. In your spiritual presence. There is no anxiety or pain in the NOW – only in the past and present.

In everything that you do, be lighter. Walk around with a lightness yet brightness of presence. Be a presence of light in a room rather than a brooding heaviness weighed down by stuff going on in your head. Allow heavy emotions and manic thoughts to evaporate into the air above you.

If your mind sounds like the dark engine room deep down in a huge ship, throw open the windows and expose it to the light around you.

If you are walking around thinking "Life is terrible" or "I am so depressed", try disconnecting yourself from the self you are observing and realise that the woe and heaviness is actually just your mind grown out of control.

When you find yourself brooding or over-worrying or lamenting, realise that your thinking mind is just a tool that is out of control, and you *can* switch it off. Reducing the size and activity of your mind will take some work, but it *will* work if you try it.

Perhaps to some extent we are even scared of the true lightness of our being – as we might be scared of a bright light or an angel appearing above us. But if you open your mind to the light you will be blessed by its presence.

Your Money and Your Work

Eureka No. 28

You won't earn more than you do today until you see yourself as worth more

According to the best-selling author of *Secrets of the Millionaire Mind*, T. Harv Eker, we all have our 'money thermostat' set at a certain level. Some people see themselves as £20,000 a year earners, some as £50,000 a year, some as £200,000 a year and so on.

Whatever your thermostat is currently set at, you're unlikely to start earning more than that unless you make a concerted effort to reset it. If you see yourself as an average earner driving an old car and never being able to afford what some of your friends can, then that's probably how you'll be. If you concentrate every day on images of yourself earning more than your friends and living in a house with a gravel drive, then that's more likely to be what happens to you in the end. In fact, take a look at most wealthy people and you can guarantee that they didn't get wealthy by accident – they actively planned, sought and lived for that dream.

This theory is also in step with the increasignly popular idea of the Laws of Attraction and the idea of 'The Secret'. The basic idea here is that whenever we think about something, focus on something or put our energy into it, the more likely we are to get that into our lives. On a health level, for example, this is seen in the placebo effect where merely believing we are going to feel better can make us do so. Likewise, if our thoughts are always negatively focused on things that annoy us or are against us, then that's going to be the lot we'll get.

A lot of our programming, of course, happened when we were younger. Many of us form an idea quite early on about how our lives are going to turn out and our relationship with wealth and money forms a big part of that. So working out what our current restricting beliefs are is a good place to start.

Ask yourself what you feel about people who earn a lot of money? How do you feel about the amount you earn? How much do you think you are worth? What was your parents' outlook on money? Questions like these will help you get a clearer idea about your current 'money thermostat' and relationship with wealth.

Then, once you've sorted out a bit of background information, you can start using the power of the Law of Attraction in your life. Your main aim here is to have a strong, vivid and specific idea about what you want. You then need to focus your positive attention on believing that you are going to get it. Many of us do the reverse of this, in fact, by focusing on what we DON'T want but attracting that to ourselves in the process.

An example that Rhonda Byrne gives in her book, *The Secret. "Most people have a goal of getting out of debt. That will keep you in debt forever. Whatever you're thinking about, you will attract. You say, "But it's get out of debt." I don't care if it's get out or get in, if you're thinking debt, you're attracting debt. Set up an automatic debt repayment program and then start focusing on prosperity."*

Start living your life as is you already have what you want instead of focusing on what you do or don't have right now or what you'd like to get away from. Visualise your new future on a daily basis.

One thing to note here, of course, is that what you may actually find you already have what you want, and that you can actually stop wishing for something different. Put it another way, be careful what you wish for!

Eureka No. 29

Change your life dramatically by looking for a NEW JOB – with a higher salary, a more fulfilling role or just a refreshing change of scene

Most of us stay put in the same job far longer than we need to – and often far longer than is good for our career.

In fact, many of us only look for a new job when we lose our old one or can't bear it a day longer, even when we're unhappy, unsatisfied and underpaid. Yet we are often suffering unnecessarily, while a far better job is waiting just around the corner.

Start looking around for a new job and there's a good chance you'll find a better paid one – whether it's in the same field or a new one where your skills can be optimised. And if you're currently unhappy in your job, then a new, happier or more meaningful work environment or challenge could be just what you're looking for.

If you find yourself having reservations about this idea or avoiding it then ask yourself why. If it's because you love the job you're in now and don't want to change, then that's brilliant. If it's your own abilities or desirability you're doubting, then surely it's at least worth trying. You may be pleasantly surprised by just how employable you are.

The most likely reason, however, is that as a human being you simply don't like change – or can't be bothered to make the effort compared to staying in the comfort of the status quo.

According to Richard Nelson Bolles in *What Colour is Your Parachute* (the best-selling job hunting book in the world, apparently!), the five most successful methods of trying to find a job are (in increasingly powerful order):

1. To ask people you know or meet, including family members and friends, people in the community and staff at career or education centres.

2. To apply directly to any employer, company, department or shop that interests you.
3. Use the phone book to *"identify subjects or fields of interest to you in the town or city where you are, and then call up the employers listed in that field to ask if they are hiring for the type of position you can do, and do well."*
4. As in No.3 but in a group with fellow job-hunters.
5. Take the *Creative Approach to Job Hunting or Career-Change* as outlined in Richard Nelson Bolles' book. What this basically entails is doing an inventory of yourself and your skills, creatively researching what you'd like to do, then working out how best to get a job where you want to work.

All these methods have a far higher chance of success than applying for a job you see advertised, or relying on an agency to find you a job.

Career-change guru Valerie Young says "My own personal wake-up call came when my mother died unexpectedly at age 61. She died too young – just five months shy of her long-awaited retirement to Florida. Losing my mother was the hardest thing I think I've ever experienced. Her own dreams deferred, I realized I could no longer put my own on hold."

So did Valerie decide that saving for a pension was a waste of time, cash in her savings and travel around the world? No. She realised that it was time to start making the most of her life NOW, to take control of her life…to make it go in the direction she chose. Although that certainly didn't mean choosing to make less money.

In fact, it is often when we actually move our working life up a gear and take control of it ourselves, that we actually move our earning capacity or mode to a different level.

Eureka No. 30

All you need to realise your dreams of more wealth is a definite PLAN and a POSITIVE ATTITUDE

We're all very good at WISHING we were richer. Barely a day passes when we don't spend some time thinking about it. In fact, the act of wishing we were richer seems to be as fundamental to our being human as having a pancreas. The desire for material wealth and security – for good or bad – is part of the human nature and will to survive.

But how far exactly does this wishing get us?

Merely wishing you could get wealthy probably has something like a 1 in a million success rate. Actually doing something definite and concerted about it has a much higher probability. And no, buying a lottery ticket every week doesn't count as making a plan for greater wealth I'm afraid.

Remember, nothing in your life is likely to suddenly change that much unless you do something to make it happen. You won't become a famous author unless you sit down and write a brilliant book. You won't become enormously wealthy unless you actually get down to it and start your own business. Your current business won't grow bigger and bigger unless you are constantly and enthusiastically looking for new ways to grow it.

Richard Carlson, life coach and best-selling author, has a theory that he has tested on many clients over the years and found consistently to be generally true and always useful: People who set aside one hour every day for the question "How can I earn more money?" inevitably reach a high level of accumulated wealth after just two years of consistent application of this method.

So how can you get started? By getting started, of course!

It may take some time, and trial and error before you arrive at a definite and successful plan that's going to turn your life around or increase your income. Your route to a more positive and financially rewarding working life may also come in stages and take some interesting turns and changes. But NOTHING will happen unless you knuckle down to THINKING… PLANNING… and then actually ACTING.

Start with baby steps and you'll be amazed at where the simple act of getting the ball rolling may take you.

When starting to make your plan, think of it as a two year plus project. Why? Because most people overestimate what they can achieve in two months but underestimate what they can achieve in two years. If you hope to accomplish too much too quickly you will get demotivated by how little progress you're making. A good plan also needs to have plenty of room to accommodate all the steps you may need in it. And amazing things can be achieved in that timescale.

In two years time you could be doing your boss's job, earning an income that now only seems a dream… or running a highly successful multi-million pound company!

Be POSITIVE about possibilities, your own abilities and your new brilliant future. Whatever you do, never forget that ideas are very delicate things. If you start showering them with negativity as soon as they are born they will very quickly whither and die. Be positive and persistent about any wealth-increasing ideas you come up with. Give them time to expand and take shape before you start even thinking about potential problems. Imagine your life panning out exactly how you would love it to – without any reservations or disbeliefs coming in and making you think it isn't possible.

Do not scrimp on time or energy spent exploring the possibilities. Remember, this is the rest of your life we're talking about, the only one you'll ever have. This may be the best investment of time you ever make.

Eureka No. 31

There are 4 key Eureka Strategies for increasing how much you earn...

1. **Ask for or work towards a pay rise or promotion.** The fastest way to go about earning more money is to go to your boss right away and tell them that you're not entirely happy with where you are or how you're progressing.

   If you're going to do this, then you need to come armed with justifications for why you should be promoted or given a pay rise – and this means showing why you *deserve* it, rather than why you need it! Talk about all the things you've done for the company recently. Talk about what more you'd like to be able to give and explain why you think you can do it.

   Alternatively, you can plan to talk to your boss about it at your next arranged pay review, or at a time in, say, 6 months' time when you will be ready with a more convincing case. Then start exceeding what is required from you, and actively find ways that you can make yourself more indispensable. If you work in an organisation that makes profits, do your best to increase profits for your company. Show plenty of enthusiasm, be pleasant and positive, and keep a note of all the great things you've done.

2. **Look for a new job.** Most people tend to stay in the same job until something serious pushes them into leaving. Seeking better-paid work while you're currently in employment, however, is an under-used method for raising your salary. See Eureka No. 29 for good pointers here.

3. **If you're self-employed, think of ways to expand your business.** Take, for example, a man who has been working as an electrician for the past few years. He is already working almost every hour of the day, so he presumes his earning capacity is already at its limit.

But what if he was to take on another electrician, do more advertising, and double the size of his business? Or could he look for ways of earning more for each hour's work, taking and drumming up more of the kind of business where he can charge more for his services?

Obvious but often under-exploited ways of expanding your business include better marketing and targeting, employing others, diversifying the business, and simply charging more.

4. **Develop a second stream of income or start a new business.** There are, of course, many possibilities here. This new stream could be connected to your current work or be completely different. It could remain a small contribution or even one day overtake your current job and replace it.

   A second stream of income could also mean doing extra work on the side, such as drain clearing, curtain making, or teaching evening classes. It could mean taking on a second employer or starting a small business or project for yourself. Your current job or your hobbies are often a good place to start looking for money-making ideas. Beginning with something you know can have a greater chance of success than launching into something too ambitious and unfamiliar. Or you could simply replicate a business model that you know is working somewhere else.

   In her book, *The Millionaire Maker*, for example, business woman Loral Langemeier, says "The key to finding the right venture is to pick a skill set that you could use to create revenue within a week, even if I pick you up and place you anywhere in the country. That's a cash machine."

   One example she gives is of a man who she helped turn his hobby making dune buggies into a $50K a year business. Another example is of a woman who made a business selling educational toys for kids through house parties after she had trouble getting hold of these items herself.

   What kind of a business? One standard blueprint for a large percentage of business ideas is to buy something for a low price and sell it for a higher price. E-bay and the internet in general are obviously good places to sell, but you could also think of other venues such as house parties or selling door-to-door. Another way of earning money is to sell SERVICES. For example, helping people do things they can't, don't want to, or don't have time to do themselves. A new business I've noticed, recently, for example, is an oven-cleaning service.

Make money by making the world a better place. Those who make the most money are often the ones who have a burning passion to give something to other people – or a vision of the world that is bigger and braver than anyone else's. Henry Ford wanted to make motor cars so cheaply that every family in the country would be able to afford one. Bill Gates wanted to put a computer into every home. JK Rowling wanted to write stories that would entertain and delight her children better than any that she found available.

One particular area worth investigating at the moment is the need for more environmentally friendly products. As the American businessman, Joseph Sugarman said, "Each problem has hidden in it an opportunity so powerful that it literally dwarfs the problem." Could you become wealthy by starting up a shop that sells only locally-produced goods? Could you find a profitable use for some of the million tonnes of different kinds of rubbish and no-longer wanted goods that we are currently throwing away?

Could you become the first car dealership in your town selling only environment-friendlier vehicles? Could you set up a business in the Congo that would improve the lives of the thousands of young children currently working 12 hours a day in copper mines?

Eureka No. 32

The secret of financial happiness is to find contentment in what you have right now

Longing for more is the biggest source of discontentment and misery

According to the extensive 'Conditions of Happiness' surveys carried out by Ruut Veenhoven, one of the main causes of unhappiness in life is desire for greater wealth. Wherever there is an unrequited desire for anything, in fact, dissatisfaction and unhappiness is created.

In fact, as hundreds of studies have now shown, the amount of wealth you own actually has little bearing on your levels of wellbeing and happiness – unless you are living in very bad poverty, or you're noticeably less well off than everyone else around you.

The secret of happiness, some even say, is finding contentment and joy in what you have right now. In the family members you adore. In the trees on your way to work. Or just in the fact that you are alive.

Living in a consumer society where beautiful material possessions are constantly paraded in front of our nose and foisted upon us by advertising, it is easy to become obsessed with what we don't have and forget what we do. Take a look around your home and your life, and appreciate all the beautiful things that you own or have access to already. Handle some of the ornaments, clothes and the knick knacks that you have, and realise how exquisite they are.

For a child living in a mud hut in Ethiopia, playing football with a ball made of rags is an enormous source of joyful pleasure and laughter. A sparkling new ball would seem like the richest of possessions. Yet give a child from the West such a gift for Christmas and they might just ask you what else you've got them.

"Possessions," said the philosopher Friedrich Nietzsche, "are generally diminished by possession." The more we have, the more we want in other words – unless we make a conscious effort to be happy with what we have.

Anxiety about money, of course, is a serious source of unhappiness for many of us. And with escalating costs, this seems harder and harder to avoid. One solution, of course, is to realise that we only create more anxiety for ourselves by allowing our outgoings to outstrip our income, and that cutting down on the former can take a lot of pressure off our lives – whether it means just foregoing the mobile phone or downsizing our home. It may also be helpful to create ourselves a mental safety net by asking ourselves what is the worst that can happen to us? Would you not find happiness wherever you were if you understand that the best riches in life are free? And would you not perhaps enjoy rising to the challenge and finding happiness in adversity?

Eureka No. 33

The secret wealth-accumulation formula of *The Millionaire Next Door*

How to accumulate wealth and security instead of spending everything you've got

Which of the people you see around you in your town are the really wealthy ones?

Part of that, of course, depends on what you call wealth. In our easy credit, consumer society we are more likely to judge people's wealth levels these days on the kind of house they live on, the car they drive, and how much they spend on a bottle of wine or bouquet of flowers… rather than how much money they have in the bank or whether they actually own the home they live in or it's a 95% mortgage.

In researching for their book, *The Millionaire Next Door*, authors Thomas J. Stanley and William D. Danko surveyed more than 11,000 wealthy people in America to discover what it was that set them apart from others. What they found was astonishing.

While all of the millionaires they surveyed had over a million dollars in savings or assets, the majority of them lived very un-wealthy lives, choosing to live well below their means. They generally lived in very ordinary neighbourhoods, in very ordinary houses, and drove very ordinary cars. And this careful thrift was exactly how they had managed to get wealthy in the first place.

On the other hand, there were a lot of people interviewed for the survey who lived in expensive houses, wore expensive clothes, drove expensive cars and yachts. But they actually OWNED very little and OWED a lot more.

Sure, given the income they had, they could have been as wealthy as the millionaires. But they chose to live super-luxury lifestyles and spend everything they earnt.

If your aim is to be able to live a life of high levels of material luxury, then this particular eureka is not for you. Bear in mind, however, that as philosopher Arthur Schopenhauer observed, “Wealth is like seawater: the more we drink, the thirstier we become.”

If the idea of financial security and an accumulation of wealth as you get older is one that appeals to you, then this simple formula is a very effective one. The idea is that the more you can do in each of the steps the better. Increasing your efforts in at least two areas will go a long way as well.

Step 1: Earn more money if you feel that your income is not sufficient. If you are using your natural talents to contribute well to life then you should be well rewarded for what you’re doing. See Eureka no. 31 for more details here.

Step 2: Hold onto more of the money you earn instead of letting it all go on taxes or credit deals for cars you can’t actually afford. One factor to bear in mind here, for example, is that as our incomes slowly increase over the years, so does our spending. As soon as we can afford it, we start eating in more expensive restaurants, buying more expensive presents and shopping in Waitrose rather than Tescos. If we keep hold of some of the money-saving habits we had when we were less well off, however, we can afford to put more by and pay off more of our mortgage and start accumulating for the future.

Step 3: Invest as much as you can in proven effective ways that will bring you both satisfaction and enjoyment now and in the future. Obvious ways of investing your money are in stock market investments, bonds and high interest accounts. But there are also more potentially lucrative, fun and creative ways of making the money you have now grow. When property prices are low, then buying property can offer very high returns and a buildup of assets. Investing in new businesses is also one of the main ways that wealthy people grow their wealth exponentially. For other assets that you can enjoy now but hopefully see hold onto their value, think of things like art and antiques. A 17th century chair is more likely to hold its value, for example, than if you spent the same money on a state of the art television or a new Chanel party frock.

Eureka No. 34

Earn more money – by being more of yourself

Wouldn't it be nice not to flinch when you open up the gas bill or the car needs new tyres? Wouldn't it be nice to see your bank account £5,000 in the black instead of £700 in the red? Wouldn't it be nice to have enough to help a friend or a sibling out with a £10,000 cash gift without it breaking the bank?

Surely, I ask you, it's not asking for too much. It's not being greedy. **But is there, perhaps, a part of you, that would feel guilty about having more than you do today?** Would that make you feel like a bad person? Or would that even, perhaps, put too much strain on the question of your worth or whether what you've done (and who you are) has been good enough to earn it?

Do not be so modest. You have so much more to offer this world than you will admit, even to yourself. Do not feel bad about feeling you are great, but rather realise that it is your duty in life to GIVE more of your own particular kind of greatness.

If you love being yourself then your aim is to be even more of you. And the more you let yourself be, the more money you can make.

We all have something special that we can give to the world. Find what that is and do not be shy of giving more of it.

I seriously believe that you can make the pursuit of 'wealth' a life-affirming activity. If the problem you face right now is how to get £500,000 in the bank, then your journey there should be a life-enhancing, self-celebrating, world-loving adventure that not only celebrates your own individuality but also adds to your union with this world.

Even if we are all only tiny specks in the Universe, we should still all aspire to be good specks!

Not that I am saying money is everything, of course. If your Number One priority in life is to live life well, then money will naturally take on less of an importance for you and your rewards will come in enjoying what you have and finding bounty in everything.

If you desire primarily money then you will miss out on life. But if you are frightened of money then you are perhaps frightened of life too.

As Mae West said, “Too much of a good thing can be wonderful.”

Eureka No. 35

Make sure you NEVER lose your job: Make yourself INDISPENSABLE and 110% employable

For many people, "work" is something they do with some reluctance. It therefore goes without saying that they will tend to do a 'good enough' job not to be given the push or annoy their bosses. Even if we work for ourselves we tend to do a 'good enough' job to keep business going and make enough money to cover the bills and pay for the annual holiday.

But is 'good enough' always good enough to safeguard our job? Will it line us up for a pay increase or promotion… or move us up to a higher level of earning?

If you're worried about keeping hold of a job during a recession then the Number One thing you can start doing today is to try each and every day to do better than just 'good enough'.

You need to take time to think about what you can do to ensure you become as indispensable as possible to your employers and or your customers. What can you do to go the extra mile… to make your bosses life easier… to improve the profits of the business… or to make those you come into contact with say "That person is really good"?

Now is the time to make sure you stand out in your company. Enjoy the chance to shine and show energy and creativity just as everyone else is crippling themselves with worry and fear about the future.

If at all possible, make sure you are an important part of actually bringing money in to your company. Make sure the important people realise that if cuts are to be made, you should be one of the last ones to go. Make sure you are crucial and indispensable and seen as competent and hard working. Get to work early, leave late, work hard and most importantly, make sure people notice.

Instead of making your employers think you're good enough – aim to make them think 'wow'.

Eureka No. 36

Setting yourself goals can DOUBLE your achievement rate AND happiness!

One of the best ways of ensuring that you perform really well is to set yourself goals. In one of the many studies that have proven this, for example, a group of young children were asked to jump over a bar. The control group managed to jump the bar an average of 3.8 times. The children with specific goals, however, jumped the bar an amazing 6.9 times.

In another study from 1997, task-specific goal-setting for pizza delivery drivers not only improved their performance of the specific tasks themselves, but also for other behaviors not targeted!

In a further study of Harvard Business School students, only 3% were found to be setting themselves clear written goals. Ten years later those 3% of students were earning ten times the other 97% combined.

Whether you want to lose weight, get a promotion, learn how to mountain climb or become a millionaire, you can increase your chances of achieving by setting yourself goals that are:

a) Specific;
b) Manageable but yet sufficiently demanding;
c) Within a realistic but yet sufficiently tight time scale.

If your goals are non-specific or too difficult, you will probably doom yourself to failure. Set them just right, however, and it could be your ticket to success.

Let's say, for example, that your goal is to lose weight. Setting yourself a goal such as "I will lose 10 pounds in two months by walking to work every Tuesday and Thursday and eating 30% less chocolate" is far more like to work than "I will lose a stone in a month by eating a lot less".

If your aim is to increase profits for your company, then your goal may be something like “I will increase profits by 5% over the next six months by finding 5 ways of cutting costs”.

If your aim is to get hold of some extra cash for yourself, your goal might be something like “I will make £300 by selling off my old books and records by 15th August” or “I will make an extra £2,000 in the next six months by following as many suggestions as I can in the book about 500 ways to boost your income.”

If you would really like to increase the amount of time you spend with the children, your goal may be “By the end of next month I will spend half an hour extra with my children twice every week by asking my boss if I could start half an hour earlier and leave half an hour earlier on those days. If my boss refuses then I will arrange an activity that we can all do regularly together at the weekends.”

Eureka No. 37

How to get almost anyone to do almost anything – from improving your children's behaviour to making an interviewer give you a job

It is a strange trait in human beings that we somehow expect to be able to get others to do what we want them to do, simply because *we* want it. It is far more effective, however, to get others to act in a certain way or do a certain thing because *they* want to do it.

One effective way of getting others to do what you would like them to is by showing them how it will *benefit them*. In order to do this, you need to find out what it is that they *want* and show them how they can get it by doing what you suggest.

If you are keen to persuade an employer to take you on, for example, you need to pay special attention to finding out what they're looking for. Then tell them you can deliver it. If you want to persuade your boss to give you more responsibility, then you need to show them how it will benefit them to do so.

Another highly effective way of influencing people is to get them to copy others. It has been shown, for example, that when badly behaved or socially-challenged children are shown videos of children behaving or functioning well, they quickly adapt and learn new ways of playing and integrating with others.

The key is to decide what kind of behaviour you'd like a person to adapt. Then put them in a situation where they will be able to see the desired behaviour being exhibited by others. This will work most effectively if the person is able to see what rewards or benefits the other person is getting from adapting this behaviour as well.

Eureka No. 38

Be the best at everything you do – by seeking constructive *criticism* instead of praise

It's a wonderful feeling to do a job well and hear people congratulate you on what you have done. It is human nature to look for praise. But if you want to do even better, if you want to improve and grow, the best way to do it is to ask for criticism, not praise.

With everything from your bolognaise sauce to your role at work or as a spouse… you could be doing an even better job if you ask others how you could improve. Of course, I'm not saying that you should walk around encouraging people to tell you that you're rubbish or that they'd rather eat a bowl of gruel in a basement than come to your house for dinner. If you're looking for praise in the first place then you must already at least half believe that what you've done or the way you do things is pretty good already.

So rather than asking, "Do you like this?" "Was that good?" or "Am I a good mother?", try asking questions like "What do you think I could do to make this better?", "What more do you think I could do?" or even "What do you think is wrong with X, Y or Z?" instead.

Not only will this help you excel further in what you do, you may actually be surprised to discover that this will give you MORE confidence in yourself. **Instead of relying on the praise of others to prop up your ego or sense of self-worth, you're having the courage, confidence and fundamental belief in yourself to grow even further.**

Of course, you do need to have a certain level of resilience to cope with this. But the key is to remember that these are ideas for making things even better – not an opportunity for the other person to completely decimate your character. Choose your person and question carefully and you should hopefully get a helpful mixture of both truthful praise and thoughtful appraisal. It could also do a lot for your relationship with the person you ask.

Prepare for a few shocks along the way, and remember: You can always reject any criticism you receive if you believe it to be wrong.

Another alternative if this sounds too risky, is to carry out an honest appraisal yourself. This way, you can ensure that you're really pushing yourself to achieve as high a level as you're capable of.

Human nature means that most of us are happy to do a good enough job. Left to our own auto-pilot devices, we will choose the path of least resistance and minimum effort. But if we really put our minds to it and decide to try even harder, we can take a look at most things that we do and work out things we could be doing better. It is just a case of applying a little more thinking and a little more effort – and blocking out the voice that tries to persuade you that good enough will do.

So ask yourself questions such as:

"What could I do on a day to day basis to contribute more to the company I work for – or the environment I work in?"

"What could I do to give more support and happiness to my husband?"

"How could I cope better with my role as mother?"

Split your personality in two and give one free rein to appraise and improve the other, and you'll be amazed at the zeal with which your critical self takes on the task.

Eureka No. 39

It is our job to give meaning to our life – rather than expecting our work or life to give meaning to us

Keep on wondering what it's all about? Feel that your life has no meaning? Stuck in a meaningless job?

Then let me ask you a few questions:

First of all, what *would* it look like for your life to have more meaning?

What would a job need to be like in order for it to be meaningful?

What would you need to do to make your life feel more meaningful?

And finally, what would it look like for the world to actually have meaning for you? Gets you thinking, doesn't it? And the important thing might be that you can't expect to find this 'meaning' unless you have a clear idea of what this 'meaning' is that you're looking for.

It is not the world that gives meaning to us, but rather we that give it meaning. You should not expect your job to give meaning to you, but rather aim to add meaning to your job. Meaning is something human beings put into the world. So if you've been looking to take it out then you've probably been going about it the wrong way.

Meaning is something you should seek to create – whether in the small things you do during your day, or through a larger mission you may find in life.

In his book, *Stepping Up*, priest and business coach Timothy Dobbins says that "In the average day, we may have a dozen different chances to make a difference. On the rush-hour drive to work we can allow someone to merge into our lane or we can force her to wait. On our way to the office we can ignore the man in the company cafeteria from whom we buy a cup of coffee or we can step up and smile and wish him a good day."

Throughout every day, says Timothy Dobbins, there are literally hundreds of moments where we have different options about how we can act. And we could all do with being a little more aware of how we can make a difference to this world by choosing the better (and often braver) options.

So how about you? What actions can you take to add more shine, depth, goodness or meaning to life? How could you give more of you at work (your strengths, your skills, your positive attributes) to make a big difference to what goes on there? Is there something you'd rather be doing instead, somewhere you would be able to contribute more?

Sometimes when we say 'meaning' we are thinking of other things, such as involvement with life, feeling in the flow of it, believing that it is good. We may feel somehow outside of it.

As the novelist Henry Miller said, *"The moment one gives close attention to anything, even a blade of grass, it becomes a mysterious, awesome, indescribably magnificent world in itself."* Get close enough up to life and it will breathe its meaning into you.

"I am a camera with its shutter open, quite passive, recording not thinking. Recording the man shaving at the window opposite and the woman in the kimono washing her hair."

From Goodbye Berlin, Christopher Isherwood

"The question of meaning in life is, as the Buddha taught, not edifying. One must immerse oneself into the river of life and let the question drift away."

Irvine Yalom, author and eminent psycotherapist

Your Health and Longevity

Eureka No. 40

[illegible] unexplained symptoms or conditions? As many as [illegible] of [illegible] could be caused by an intolerance to certain foods.

[illegible]

[illegible]

[illegible]

What are the symptoms of a food intolerance?

The [illegible] symptoms of food intolerance include headache and migraine, [illegible] depression, anxiety, asthma, muscle or joint pains, eczema and [illegible] problems with your skin, mouth ulcers, weight gain, [illegible] and a whole range of digestive problems.

This list is [illegible] far from exhaustive and it is perhaps more accurate to say that it's possible to suffer from any symptom or combination of symptoms that your doctor has been unable to fix. It is most CERTAINLY worth investigating whether a food intolerance could be the cause [illegible]

Many overweight people – particularly men – may also find that the problems they have with shifting weight are partly or entirely down to an intolerance to carbohydrate.

Eureka No. 40

Undiagnosed or uncured symptoms or conditions? As many as 45% of our ills could be caused by an intolerance to certain foods...

Could your headaches be caused by an intolerance to chicken? Could giving up milk make all your health symptoms vanish? Could an intolerance to certain foods even be causing your asthma or arthritis?

You'd better believe it. Around 45% of the population suffer some kind of adverse reaction to food, according to Allergy UK, the UK's leading medical charity for people with allergies, food intolerance and chemical sensitivities.

Food intolerance has now been linked to dozens of different symptoms and even serious conditions such as asthma, eczema, Crohn's disease, depression, migraines and irritable bowel syndrome. Yet it is still unlikely that your doctor will even mention the possibility of a food intolerance to you when you present your problem.

So what are the symptoms of a food intolerance?

The main symptoms of food intolerance include headache and migraine, fatigue, depression or anxiety, aching muscles or joints, rheumatoid arthritis, problems with your skin, mouth ulcers, weight gain, nausea and stomach ulcers and a whole range of digestive problems.

This list, however, is far from exhaustive and it is perhaps more accurate to say that if you suffer from any symptom or combination of symptoms that your doctor has been unable to fix, it is most CERTAINLY worth investigating whether a food intolerance could be the cause of it.

Many overweight people – particularly men – may also find that the problems they have with shifting weight are partly or entirely down to an intolerance to carbohydrate.

What foods are the biggest food culprits?

You can develop a sensitivity to almost any food – and in many cases of intolerance, more than one culprit may be involved. The different foods eaten in large quantities in different countries tend to be the biggest culprits. In the UK, for instance, milk and wheat are the first two suspects. It is quite possible, however, that if you suffer from an intolerance to these two, there may be a few more 'culprits' on your list of inedible foods.

Other top culprits include nuts, peanuts, eggs, shellfish, oranges, coffee, alcohol, sugar, yeast and additives… and also any foods that you find yourself particularly craving.

So what can you DO?

The most scientific way of finding out whether you have a food intolerance is by following a very strict elimination diet. While some of the tests you may find for sale on the internet or in health food shops etc may perhaps give results that could be useful, there is no definite proof that any of them are anywhere near as scientific or conclusive as they claim. The results may be right – but then again they may not.

An elimination diet is not really a 'diet' at all – but a diagnostic test. This is not a way of solving your problems, but of finding out what the source of your problems might be. Basically, it involves eliminating all foods that could possibly be causing you a problem. It puts you on a diet of the remaining "allowed" foods for two or three weeks – or until you feel better, depending on which is sooner.

This is called the "exclusion" phase of the diet. After that, you then reintroduce all the potential offenders, one at a time, for one week each. This is what is known as the "reintroduction" phase. If a food intolerance is to blame for your symptoms, they will reappear when the culprit food is introduced.

Is there an easier way?

If you suspect that food intolerance may be a problem, but you're not quite ready to throw yourself into the deep end with a full elimination diet, then you may prefer to try a few mini-tests first. These small tests may be enough to solve your problem sufficiently alone. Alternatively, they may offer enough of a breakthrough to encourage you to take the elimination diet one step further.

Start, for example, by going entirely without any dairy products for a week or two then eat it a lot for a whole day and compare what happens. Bear in mind if you do this that you may actually feel worse initially if you deprive your body of your culprit food. Your symptoms, however, should begin to feel much better by the end of the first week – giving you inspiration to try it for the next week too.

After that (and it is probably worth trying other foods as well even if your first attempt hits the spot), move onto wheat – going without all foods that contain it (including bread, pasta, biscuits, pastry and beer). After that, you can move on to other offenders on the 'top culprit' list.

Another option is to keep a food diary for a week. You may find, for example, that your headaches seem to occur when you eat foods high in additives… that your joint pain is less on days when you don't eat potatoes… or that your digestive problems ease up on days when you don't eat that midday sandwich.

Also worth noting is that food intolerances can work in conjunction – or even be caused and worsened by – emotional, physical or environmental influences. These include stress, illness, an impaired immune system, inadequate nutrition, nutritional deficiencies (including deficiencies caused by over-consumption of alcohol, sugar and or caffeinated drinks, environmental pollution, toxic overload, and smoking).

Eureka No. 41

Flood your body with powerful natural endorphins to remove stress, soothe pain and heal your illnesses and inner instability

"The greatest reassurance and safety that can be given to your body is the warm attention of your own mind."

Endorphins are a powerful hormone naturally produced by the body to remove pain and stress and to enhance and aid the work of immunological processes. The more they are allowed or encouraged to flow in our bodies, the happier and healthier we can be. Yet our modern lifestyles and outlook to our bodies often have the effect of actually preventing these hormones from flowing.

In his brilliant book, *The Endorphin Effect*, holistic teacher Dr. William Bloom shows how increasing the amount of the hormones called endorphins in our body can be a major key to better health, better mind, increased joy and less pain. Endorphins can be produced at any location in the body and can flow through the whole body like waves in an ocean. Once you've experienced being able to increase the flow in yourself, it's a powerful boost you can give yourself at any time of the day.

For many of us, the most important thing we need to correct is the disconnected state in which we live most of our lives. We spend a lot of our time disconnected from the world around us and disconnected from our bodies. We live in an isolated bubble of our own fraught ego and mind instead of living in our bodies and within nature.

To reconnect with the world and increase your sense of inner stability, it is often enough, says Dr. Bloom, for people to do something as simple as "pausing to recognise where they are physically located. In the centre of the city or in the buzz of their office, they pause to notice the sky and position of the sun. They orient themselves to the points of the compass and know the direction in which their home is located."

"To persons standing alone on a hill during a clear midnight such as this, the roll of the world eastward is almost a palpable movement."

Thomas Hardy, Far From the Madding Crowd

Reconnecting with your body (not just now but every day and through the day) can be as simple as just tuning into it and caring for it a little more. Focus your mind on parts of your body or your body as a whole and send it messages of warmth, comfort and illumination.

In William Bloom's words: "To create stability, confidence and strength, you must have a firm awareness of your body. Without this attention, your body is always hyped up to go automatically into instinctive biological defence and survival mechanisms. Tension means to be in a continuous state of frightened preparation, ready to flood yourself with the energy of adrenalin. The result of this is a constant readiness for the three Fs – Flight, Fight or Fright. Because of this, some people are in a perpetual state of depression, low level anger and frustrated aggression.

"If you give your body affectionate attention it is reassured that, despite all the external noise, you are still aware of it and caring for it. Every time you send it the Inner Smile, you will experience a tangible change in the way that you feel. Your body is like a child holding your hand in dangerous traffic. Give it reassuring signals and it will feel safe."

Another great way of giving yourself extra little shots of endorphin pleasure throughout the day is to think of things that give you pleasure, things that make you feel stronger, or things that connect you with the wonder and beauty of life beyond your current situation.

If you are prepared to invest the time, it can help enormously to create a list of such endorphin-enhancing thoughts that you can use whenever you need them. These can include places that make you feel good… people, pets or animals… objects or effects from nature such as dew on a spider's web or frost on a window… activities you have done… fond memories you cherish… spiritual or religious thoughts… or even colours, sounds or textures such as the feel of the softest velvet or the taste of a fresh minted potato.

Eureka No. 42

Ever wondered whether your pain or illness could be linked to an emotional or psychological influence?

Just reading these words below could make your symptoms start to vanish...

It seems today that more and more doctors are using the handy label "stress-related" to explain dozens of conditions they can't cure. But from headaches and skin problems to digestive problems and high blood pressure, is this word "stress" really enough to explain what might be going on – and to help us get to the bottom of it?

The first thing to note when exploring the idea of psychosomatic illness is that when we say an illness or pain is psychosomatic, we do NOT mean that it is "all in the mind" or merely imagined. If a physical problem is caused by or linked to a cognitive or emotional phenomenon, it is as physically real as a broken leg caused by a fall or the swelling caused by an insect bite.

The problem with emotional or mental causes, of course, is that they are not as easy to identify or pinpoint as a fall down a concrete step or an angry wasp that has been sat on. The whole idea of psychosomatic illness and pain is also so new to our society that many people still find it too difficult to accept or understand how something like repetitive strain injury or chronic back pain can possibly be caused by something other than a physical or mechanical cause.

One theory: pain is created by unconscious rage

One of the leading medical pioneers in this field is Dr. John Sarno who has successfully treated many hundreds of patients suffering from chronic pain in his private practice – and has also helped many more to cure themselves through the books he has written *(Healing Back Pain and The Divided Mind)*.

What occurs in TMS (tension myositis syndrome), the name Sarno has given to the condition he has identified as afflicting hundreds of thousands of people, is that the mind creates a strong pain in the body in order to prevent the conscious mind from becoming aware of the large amount of rage occurring in the subconscious mind.

This rage may be caused by a single or combination of factors: Strong feelings or anger, sorrow or pain from childhood or other – such as life pressures, anger at aging, suppressed anger and putting unreasonable pressure on ourselves.

You are particularly likely to suffer from TMS "if you expect a great deal of yourself, if you drive yourself to be perfect, to achieve, to succeed, if you are your severest critic, if you are very conscientious, these are likely to make you very angry inside…

"The child in our unconscious doesn't care about anyone but itself and gets angry at the pressure to be perfect and good."

The first key in Dr. Sarno's self treatment programme is to simply accept that the physical symptoms are caused by emotional rage and to focus on the psychological rather than the physical. In his practice, Dr. Sarno performs a complete physical examination to reassure the patient that there is no physical cause – often having to disprove explanations that have been given to the patient by other doctors who have only been trained to offer people scientific-sounding medical explanations. Conditions like Fibromyalgia and migraine, for example, may have very credible-sounding names but that doesn't mean that doctors have much idea about their *cause*.

The second stage is to start concentrating on and exploring, *every day*, the psychological factors that you think may be contributing to your unconscious rage. Make a list, suggests Dr. Sarno, and then write about each item on your list.

Don't worry, he says – everyone has this unconscious rage. "This program is designed to stop the brain from producing pain because it fears that the rage, emotional pain, or sadness will manifest itself and be felt consciously if it doesn't do something to distract you. So you must do something to sit down and think about these things every day. This is the way the ideas get from your conscious mind to your unconscious mind.

That's where they have to get in order for the brain to stop the pain process."

Second theory: Specific emotions linked to specific pains and illnesses

Psychosomatic illness has been treated with psychotherapy since the early 20th century, the time of Sigmund Freud, and it has moved along steadily but always on the fringes. The fact that it has never made it to the main-stream does not mean that it should not. From what we have read it is often very successful. One source in particular says that it is very efficient at treating bronchial asthma, duodenal ulcers and migraine in particular.

There are now, in fact, many books that have been written about the connection between our minds and the illnesses our bodies suffer. Barbara Hobeman Levine in her book, *Your Body Believes Every Word You Say*, talks about the way our core beliefs (or "seedthoughts" as she calls them, the internal dialogues we engage in) have such a huge influence on our health.

In his book, *Sick and Tired: Healing the Illnesses That Doctors Cannot Cure*, Dr. Nick Read tells us that "between 30 and 40 per cent of people who seek health care have illnesses that have no clear cause and no obvious basis in pathology. Literally millions of people are racked by back pains, tormented by abdominal gripes, alarmed by ringing in the ears, tortured by headaches, exhausted by sleep deprivation, debilitated by nausea or faintness or anorexia". From his experience of treating thousands of such patients, Dr. Read has found that these people often suffer more anxiety or depression than others, have been through significant negative life events that they have not yet digested, have had experiences that have challenged their sense of self-worth, or tend to deny the feelings that they suffer.

None of this, of course, is completely new. Indeed, Traditional Chinese Medicine has for centuries had a system for linking specific emo-tions to specific forms of ill-health. Worry or sadness, for example, are believed to affect the health of the lungs and to cause asthma, acne, coughs and throat pain. Anger leads to headaches, dizziness and digestion problems. Too little joy in our life is bad for the heart. Excessive thought is said to cause diarrhea, indigestion and bad breath.

Exploring our own personal causes of our own personal symptoms will of course be a highly individual journey for each of us. In many cases we will be able to go a long way through self exploration. For a few, the experts believe, it may be necessary to embark on a course of psychotherapy to get to the bottom of what's going on.

And finally, to put a more down-to-earth slant on the idea, I liked this reply from *The Times* newspaper's famous doctor, Dr. Thomas Stuttaford. He is replying to a woman who wrote in saying that she felt her chronic fatigue, hormonal problems, digestive upsets and excessive weight gain etc had all been caused by problems in her life and were now getting better since her life took some changes for the better:

"This email will encourage many people. It seems that for the reader the worst is over and she has gained insight, the greatest gift that can be given to anyone with psychological or psychiatric troubles. She now understands that a period of stress can induce many varied symptoms that will only lift when some underlying problem in lifestyle has been relieved.

"Many patients with classic unipolar depressive disease, with every symptom of endogenous depression, may do well with antidepressants. But even in these patients, the final recovery and a return to their old selves only happens when some longstanding domestic or professional difficulty is removed."

Eureka No. 43

Got a health problem the doctor can't solve? Then get ready to SHOCK HIM!

How doing your own research could lead you to a Eureka cure or solution that your doctor might tell you is "impossible"

Whenever you have any kind of pain or illness, going to see your doctor should only be seen as one avenue for trying to make it better. Even the doctors we've questioned on this believe that patients who do their own research into a condition stand a better chance of finding a cure for it.

One reason for this is that with only ten minutes to see you and very little knowledge of your background, doctors may often miss something that could be crucial to finding the answer. A second reason is that with many conditions, conventional medicine only or mainly looks to treat the symptoms of a condition, rather than trying to find the underlying causes.

A third reason is that doctors often only know about mainstream, pharmaceutical approaches to treating certain conditions. You would be surprised at how little they sometimes know about alternative and complimentary medicines that have been proven highly effective.

One thing that you will probably find when you start your research – in books and on the internet – is that you may discover many different solutions or causes suggested for your condition. Don't let this put you off. The fact that a certain condition can be caused by many different triggers is one reason in fact why mainstream medicine has tended to focus on treating symptoms rather than causes. Indeed, you might even say that some of the labels that they give certain groups of conditions (asthma or migraine, for example) might actually hinder the search for a cause, rather than helping.

Hunting for a solution may mean a certain amount of trial of error and it cannot even guarantee an answer. Search the internet. Look for books in bookshops or on Amazon (you can always put them up for sale on Amazon once you've read them). Talk to the staff in your local health food shop or alternative medicines suppliers.

Below are just a few suggestions for a few conditions. Obviously this is just the tip of an enormous iceberg, but potentially the answer may be here – or certainly give you inspiration to start looking.

Asthma

Some asthma sufferers have found their asthma has been caused by fungus in the lungs, probably due to taking antibiotics a year or two before and not taking probiotics afterwards. Alternative practitioners recommend taking acidophilus once or twice a day for six weeks.

Another common irritant that can cause or aggravate asthma is mildew or dampness in the air – especially in houses where the air is constantly sealed in by double glazing.

A third theory for causes of asthma that has been enormously helpful for many is the Buteyko Breathing Method. According to the author of *Asthma-Free Naturally*, Patrick McKeown freed himself of a 20-year case of asthma using this method, and asthma can be cured in many people by teaching them to breathe through their nose, relax, and stop 'over-breathing'. If any of these questions ring a bell then you might want to consider it:

- Is your breathing a still, silent activity or does it involve large inhalations and body movements?
- Are you going about your daily activities with your mouth open?
- Do you take a big breath as you stand up from your chair or before talking?
- Do you heave big sighs, yawn or sniff regularly?
- Do you wake in the night or early morning with a dry mouth?

Alzheimer's Disease

Also for age-associated memory impairment. Try ginkgo biloba, L-carnitine, zinc and especially phosphatidylserine (PS). All have been found helpful in delaying the progression of these conditions. All worth researching further.

Arthritis

This is another condition that can be caused or aggravated by sensitivities to foods or other allergens. One woman found the cause of her suffering was a low-level gas leak from a boiler. Others believe that a general build up of noxious chemicals, viruses, bacteria, yeast and fungal infections combined with a general weakening of the immune system is to blame.

Many people find that making dietary changes can do a lot to relieve their symptoms, especially restricting meat and increasing raw vegetables and healthy foods.

When it comes to relieving the pain of arthritis, different things work better for different people. Some of the better options include MSM (methylsulfonylmethane), boswellia, cayenne pepper, lyprinol and devil's claw. Glucosamine and chondroitin are recommended for joint repair. Homeopathic remedies can also be effective for some, notably rhus toxicodendron if your symptoms get worse at night and in damp weather.

One of the most impressive supplements reported lately has been boron, with reports of very high success levels for sufferers. The supplement hyaluronic acid is not only prescribed for joint pain, but has also been found effective for reducing wrinkles!

Headaches

Headaches can have many different causes, including allergy or sensitivity (to food, drink, or dust mites for example), eyesight problems, emotional problems, tiredness, muscular tension or even eating too much salt. Many people find relief from consulting a chiropractor or craniosacral therapist.

Heart Disease

A few ideas to start your research include:

- The vitamins B6, B2, B12 (along with folic acid and zinc) – all are nutrients necessary for normalising homocysteine levels, now believed to be a key factor in heart health.
- Bonito peptides from the bonito fish are an interesting new one to research.
- The Ayurvedic herb arjuna has been used to treat heart conditions for centuries in India. Now there is great interest in the West, too.

Eureka No. 44

How just one word could revolutionize your entire health, looks and fitness and slow down the rate at which you age

If we told you there was a completely safe, amazing new medicine you could take to dramatically reduce your chances of suffering from all forms of ill health and prolong your lifespan – potentially by decades – would you take it?

And what if we also added that this life-boosting medicine could improve your mood and energy levels… make you thinner and more toned and quite probably improve your sex drive?

No, this is not a new vitamin or supplement they're touting. It's a powerful regime that need take no more than a few minutes out of your day, yet can also help improve your productivity and stamina, cure depression and even be the answer to problems like fatigue and insomnia.

What it is? *Exercise.*

We now know without any doubt that many of the age-related health problems that we suffer from (including high cholesterol, high blood pressure, insulin levels and osteoporosis risk) are directly linked to the level to which we have a SEDENTARY lifestyle.

Not to beat around the bush, the more sedentary your lifestyle, the more you are generally likely to suffer from loss of muscular strength, loss of vital capacity, poor functioning of hormones, inability to control blood sugar, reduced cognition facilities and an increase in body fat, insulin levels and stress hormones.

According to leading expert on exercise for anti-aging, Miriam E. Nelson, director of the John Hancock Center for Physical Activity and

Nutrition in Boston, “with every increasing decade of age, people become less and less active.”

“But,” Dr. Nelson says, “the evidence shows that with every increasing decade, exercise becomes more important in terms of quality of life, independence and having a full life.”

Concentrating on that word ‘sedentary’ then could be the key to supercharging your health levels. Keep moving to stay younger.

So how do you go about it?

First of all, there are few excuses for not being able to fit exercise into your day. Keeping active does not have to involve going to the gym or swimming pool or jogging round the park. Those 3-minutes while you’re waiting for the kettle to boil could be spent doing sit-ups or marching on the spot, depending on your age, current health and ability. Walk up the escalators instead of standing there like a lemon. Dance around the kitchen while you’re cooking your dinner. Do 20 star jumps or jog on the spot while you’re watching the Morrisons ad if you have to.

The key is to hunt out activities that you enjoy and to concentrate generally on being less SEDENTARY and more ACTIVE. Just moving around more and for longer is a start!

- **A crucial ingredient to staying lean is increasing your muscle strength.** Invest in a cheap set of dumb bells and put them to use while you’re waiting for your PC to turn on or as a way to rev yourself up of a morning. Even without weights you can add muscle strength to your legs simply by bending your knees until your hands reach the floor. Repeat until you tire. Take enough pride in your body to stop it from turning into fat or scrawn.
- **Walk more quickly.** Walking itself is actually sufficient exercise (along with some kind of weight-training preferably) to keep you fit. It is important, however, to walk at a fast pace if physically possible. Try singing your favourite songs or smiling as you walk and you might even feel less miserable too.
- **A flat stomach without sit-ups.** We promise you that this is the most useful thing you’ll ever read about getting a flatter stomach. When you got your body many years ago it came with special muscles

whose job it is to keep your tummy flat. Over the years, however – and perhaps as you've lost pride in your appearance – those muscles have quite probably become weaker and weaker. The easiest way to bring back strength in these muscles is to simply concentrate on pulling your stomach flat wherever you happen to be.

Imagine that you are trying to pull your belly button towards your spine with a thread coming out of your back and you should be able to feel those crucial muscles working immediately. The more you strengthen those muscles, the flatter your stomach will be. You can also do it while you're walking, while your talking and while you're standing on the train.

- **Five minute yoga exercise for flexibility.** To keep hold of your flexibility and save yourself from backache, practice the yoga routine, Salute the Sun every morning. There are plenty of good instructions about how to do this available on the internet. A particularly good and simple explanation to start with is free at www.yogasite.com/sunsalute.htm
- **Do jumping jacks** or invisible rope skipping for just two minutes a day to start experiencing results immediately.
- **Joining a dance class** (salsa, line dancing, whatever takes your fancy) is a great way to get exercise and social stimulus at the same time.
- **For easier push-ups,** push off against a wall instead of the floor.

Finally, be reassured that moderate exercise like this actually decreases your appetite for several hours afterwards.

Eureka No. 45

Protect yourself from ill health. Stay younger and live longer.

Simply add these 24 superfoods to your diet to make healthy eating so much less of a chore

The likes of Jamie Oliver and Gillian McKeith have now proven to everyone that eating the right foods instead of the wrong foods can transform your life, your happiness, your moods, your weight, your longevity, your susceptibility to disease and even your looks.

Stop the tearaway kids from eating too many sweets and they suddenly turn into calm and gentle beings. Feed a lethargic, overweight woman kidney beans and avocados, and she triples her energy levels, loses two stone, heals her diabetes and has wonderful glowing skin.

The World Health Organisation (WHO) has revealed that **85 per cent of adult cancers are entirely avoidable** and, of these, around half are related to nutritional deficiencies in the Western diet. US researchers from the Rush University Medical Centre in Chicago have found that eating two or more servings of vegetables a day can help slow the age-related decline in cognitive function by up to 40 per cent, compared with a person who consumes few vegetables (*Neurology*, 24 Oct. 2006). Another study found that people who drink one or more soft drinks a day have a more than 50 percent higher risk of developing the heart disease precursor metabolic syndrome than people who drink less than one fizzy drink a day.

The problem is, of course, that short of spending half your time reading books on nutrition and the other half in the supermarket buying the right ingredients, making sure you eat all the vitamins, minerals and super foods you need can be a logistic nightmare!

Not just a question of avoiding 'bad' foods – but adding more of the good

We're certainly not going to claim that the list of foods below is anything like a comprehensive guide to getting your nutrition perfect, but here's what we've done for you. Having spent many hours reading the top-selling books on nutrition, we've put together a list of foods that it would be really good for you to add to your diet. Our idea is that if you photocopy or type up and print out this list and stick it up in your kitchen somewhere, you'll then be able to ensure you get as many of them in your diet as often as possible and according to what your busy life allows. we've also gone for the foods that aren't too expensive – rather than the rare foods that might be great but would take up all your grocery money for the week.

We've added a few lines of reasons why these foods are great – but again, these are far from exhaustive. We've also added a few ideas about how to add them to your diet.

Avocados

Why? Great for lowering cholesterol and maintaining cardiovascular health. One recent study even found that an extract from Haas avocado was able to destroy oral cancer cells.

How? Add to salad, sandwiches or make a guacamole by mashing it up with a crushed garlic clove, some lemon or lime juice, some finely chopped tomato and either chili powder or a fresh chopped chili.

Bananas

Why? Can help prevent high blood pressure. Strengthen bones. Natural mood enhancer. Protection from stomach ulcers. High in minerals and B6.

How? Great snack for when you're hungry, on your cereal or in a smoothie.

Apples

Why? A compound in apples called procyanidin B-2 has been found to play a key role in inhibiting age-related problems, preventing wrinkles and promoting hair growth. May protect post-menopausal women from osteoporosis and may also increase bone density. Numerous studies have also shown that eating apples can help prevent many different kinds of cancer, asthma, diabetes, high blood pressure and weight gain!

How? Grab one from the bowl and munch as you go – or add to your breakfast.

Celery

Why? Reduces stress hormones. Helps with water retention. Also helps reduce the inflammation associated with conditions like arthritis.

How? In spaghetti bolognaise and risotto. Keep some sticks in an air-tight container in the fridge with a sprinkle of water, and munch as a snack whenever you're peckish.

Oily fish such as salmon, tuna and mackerel

Why? Eating oily fish as little as once a week could lower your risk of Alzheimer's by a staggering 60 per cent. Also brilliant for keeping your heart healthy and protecting you from depression.

How? From a tin or cooked fresh. Other fish are great too.

Alternative? If you are concerned by stories of "heavy metals" building up in some oily fish, add flaxseed to your diet instead.

Blueberries

Why? Extremely high in antioxidants and believed particularly effective in preventing cancer. Also help ease cystitis.

How? Buy as a treat food and eat in front of the telly instead of a packet of crisps.

Oranges

Why? Great cancer-fighting properties and very rich in nutrients.

How? I love the www.orangerecipes.org website.

Garlic

Why? Garlic contains around 200 biologically active compounds – many of which can play a role in preventing diseases including cancer and heart disease.

How? Cook with it. Make olive oil garlic bread. Roast a whole head in the oven for 45 minutes in foil and use the mild puree as a sauce or spread on bread.

Brown rice

Why? Because it's full of nutrients that you miss out on with white.

How? Takes longer to cook than white rice. Remember that it takes 30-35 minutes, so put it on early.

Oats

Why? They are high in calcium, potassium, magnesium, vitamin E, the B vitamins, protein and more. Great for the skin and for dealing with stress and tiredness. Shown to help reduce cholesterol.

How? In porridge or muesli.

Onions

Why? Onions help the body eliminate toxins and carcinogens and protect bones from osteoarthritis.

How? Get back to cooking those dishes that contain it – such as goats cheese and red onion tart.

Pineapple

Why? Especially good if you have joint problems, digestive problems or heart problems.

How? Nice for breakfast. Needs to be fresh, not tinned.

Pomegranates

Why? Great anti-everythings and better than other fruit for many nutrients.

How? Buying juices is actually better than buying the fruit!

Potatoes

Why? A better nutritional carbohydrate than white pasta, bread or rice. High in potassium, iron, B vitamins and a great source of Vitamin C as well as other antioxidants.

How? Bake (don't fry) for optimum nutrition. Sweet potatoes are even better.

Spinach

Why? Full of nutrition and great for almost every part of your body. Good protection against all kinds of conditions related to ageing.

How? Better eaten raw in salads than cooked.

Watercress

Why? Research suggests strong anti-cancer power.

How? Add to salads. Watercress soup.

Raspberries

Why? Contain a powerful anti-cancer property not found in other fruit.

How? On a pavlova, or just added to fruit salads. Frozen raspberries are cheaper and good for throwing into a smoothie from the freezer.

Tomatoes

Why? Lower the risk of prostate cancer in particular – as well as a treatment.

How? Raw or cooked anyway or in any dish. Even ketchup helps!

Broccoli (also brussel sprouts and kale)

Why? For better immunity, digestion, mood, skin and liver function.

How? Always great to boil or steam a few florets in 5 minutes as a side veg with any meal.

Nuts

Why? Great source of B Vitamins you may otherwise be lacking. Lots of health-boosting fats and nutrients. Lower your risk of heart disease.

How? A variety of different nuts is best.

Olive oil

Why? Lowers risk of heart disease and cancer. Much better for you than other oils – especially palm oil.

How? In cooking or as dressing for salad. With bread instead of butter.

Pulses

Why? Powerful anti-inflammatory and antioxidant properties. Vitamin-rich, low glycemic index and high in protein and fibre. Also great for your all-important B Vitamins.

How? Think of having beans or chick peas instead of meat or carbs. Eat in houmus, baked beans, and stews. Soy beans in particular are great for anti-cancer, menopause and PMS, and can be consumed through soya milk or Miso soup powder drink.

Wholemeal bread and pasta

Why? More nutritious and contain lots of fibre great for digestion, heart, weight and overall health.

How? Just get in the habit of reaching for a different packet at the supermarket. Even better if it contains seeds.

Pumpkin seeds

Why? Help protect you against prostate problems, osteoporosis and cancer. Anti-inflammatory and immune boosting and also effective against depression. Also contain zinc and Omega-3.

How? An alternative to snacking on crisps. Great sprinkled on your cereal or salads.

Eureka No. 46

"Smile, breathe and go slowly" like a Buddhist monk

"Breathing" said Giovanni Papini, the Italian poet and journalist, "is the greatest pleasure in life." And whenever you stop and take time during your day to become consciously aware of your deep, calm breathing, you will understand this feeling.

Whenever the mind is not calm, our breathing can also become erratic, hard or strained. Yet by calming our breathing we can also calm down our mind. Becoming aware of your breath allows you to become more aware of the beauty of just living and the world around you.

As you breathe out, imagine you are breathing out all the stresses of the day. As you breath slowly in, imagine you are filling your body with a pure white light.

"Smile, breathe and go slowly", as Thich Nhat Hanh, a Zen Buddhist monk and peace activist, put it. Or, to follow the instructions of the famous Indian yoga teacher, Krishnamacharya:

"Inhale, and God approaches you. Hold the inhalation, and God remains with you. Exhale, and you approach God. Hold the exhalation, and surrender to God."

Eureka No. 47

Lose weight by treating the causes rather than the symptom

14 medical and lifestyle causes of weight gain and how to deal with them

What do you do if you're overweight and don't want to be?

Eat less of course! Or so goes the standard thinking on the subject of weight loss.

For many people suffering from unwanted weight, however, this might be as helpful as telling a fish to stop swimming or advising a cat to get more rest. It could even be detrimental.

Sure, eating more calories than you need is probably the reason why a large number of people are overweight. But this is far from the only reason. It is also far more important to get to the bottom of the reason for overeating than to merely attempt to do the impossible.

Below is a list of 14 of the most common medical and lifestyle causes for weight gain, along with some advice about how to tackle them. For some people there may be a eureka solution here that will help them solve the problem immediately. For others there will be more of a combination of factors at play – and a more complex set of goals to work towards.

Overeating or undereating

I've put these together deliberately to highlight the potential complexity of what might be going on here – and because this is often where the whole 'eat less' idea makes people start going astray.

On one level, of course, it might just be a case that a person simply hasn't worked out or admitted to themselves yet that they eat more than they need to. Facing up to this fact may just be a practical issue, or involve a lot of soul searching.

What is often at play, however – especially for people who have been battling weight gain for some time – is that their relationship with food has gone pear shaped. Rather than just eating when they're hungry and stopping when they're full, many people get to the point where they no longer know when they need to eat and when they don't. They feel guilty about eating and obsessively crave the foods they are trying not to eat. They have a love-hate relationship with food. And they are forever trying to eat what they think they *should* rather than just eating naturally.

For a lot of people struggling to diet, it is actually the fact that they are denying themselves food that makes them put on weight. This happens because when you deny your body food that it's called for, your body goes into fat-storing mode and your metabolism slows right down.

If a naturally thin person eats say two bahjias, one samosa, three popadoms, one nan peshwari and two large helpings of chicken korma and lamb kari one night, their body will take only what it needs for energy and nutrition and eliminate the rest of the excess fat. A dieter, meanwhile, only has to look at a Weight Watchers Chicken Curry and even those three grams of fat in it go straight to their hips.

As Paul McKenna says in his best-selling diet book, *I Can Make You Thin,* "Not eating when you're hungry sets up dysfunctional patterns of thinking in the unconscious mind in relation to food. This subtle tension around food sets up a powerful neuro-chemical change in the brain that leads to false hunger signals and patterns of craving and bingeing."

So what is the answer? Learning to get back into a more natural relationship with eating and food. Eat what you want, when you want – in response to hunger. Eat happily and savor what you eat. Stop eating when you think you are full. Look to the emotional reasons tied in with your eating habits.

Genetically inclined towards overeating

Scientists have now discovered that an inability to know when we are full may be genetic. People who have little problem controlling their weight seem to have a finely tuned ability to know when they are hungry and when they have eaten sufficient. If you feel that you don't have this then it could well be down to your genetic inheritance. Once you've realised that it is this lack of appetite sensitivity that leads you to overeat, you can begin to act in accordance. If the thinner people around the table say they're full before you feel it, for example, make a note of where you too might want to stop eating!

Being too sedentary or not getting enough exercise

For many people, lifestyle changes and decreased energy levels as we age mean that we get less and less physical exercise as we get older. The fact that you're stuck at home of an evening because of the children, for example, might mean that you get a lot less exercise than you maybe used to. Increasing dependency on a car can also have a dramatic effect on your exercise levels. See Eureka No. 44 for more details on getting moving!

A diet high in carbohydrates

Fats we have been told in the past are the main cause of weight gain, and this has been partly responsible for our soaring consumption of carbohydrates instead. If you consume a lot of bread, pasta, cakes and sweet foods or drinks then this could well be your problem.

The consumption of carbohydrates leads very quickly to a rapid rise of glucose in the bloodstream. This in turn makes your pancreas produce a large amount of insulin to take the excess glucose out. Insulin is the hormone ultimately responsible for body fat storage. An intolerance or sensitivity to carbohydrates is also believed to be a key factor in weight gain – particularly for men. Try cutting down the carbohydrates in your diet and see what happens.

Eating habits that lead to overeating and weight gain

Does lunch seem incomplete without a bag of crisps? Do you always get a bag of popcorn at the cinema – or snacks in front of the telly? Have you always eaten everything that's on your plate since the days your mum told you that you have to? Has your comfort eating become more of a habitual action than something you necessarily need?

Habits, we are told, are hard to break. When it comes to eating habits, however, it is often enough to realise that we have them to enable us to knock them on the head.

Eating for comfort or to make yourself feel better when you're low

A lot of people are happy to admit that they occasionally comfort eat. Few of us are happy to even admit it to ourselves, however, if it becomes a serious problem or an addictive habit. Mainly, perhaps, because we don't want to let go of it.

Boredom, tiredness, sadness, stress and anger… these are all emotions that can lead us to treat ourselves to the serotonin rush that eating undeniably (and scientifically) affords us. Occasionally, of course, this is not a problem. When it becomes a daily habit, however, it is in some ways as powerful an addiction (and potentially as dangerous) as an addiction to heroine.

A major factor that can make it even harder to break the habit is the vicious circle effect of stimulus and guilt: You eat to feel better but then the guilt of eating makes you feel worse – even a failure in fact. Then you fill yourself again to get rid of that badness.

Another or different part of the vicious circle is the weight gain itself: The more you eat, the fatter you become. The fatter you become, the more you feel bad about yourself. The more you feel bad, the more you want to comfort eat to get rid of the pain.

So what is the solution? Like any addiction, of course, it isn't going to be easy and going turkey might be your best solution. Remind yourself that the serotonin rush you get from eating is very short-lived and will do nothing to cure the deeper down hurt. Looking to deal with that hurt and pain might be a better option. Replace your eating with other forms of endorphin stimulus (see Eureka No.41). And most importantly of all, remain aware of what you're doing.

An underactive thyroid

Otherwise known as Hypothyroidism, some sources believe that as many as one in ten women could suffer from it to some degree. In some people, thyroid hormone deficiency can decrease metabolism of food, causing appetite loss and weight gain. Weight gain is also caused by fat accumulation and fluid retention caused by protein deposits in the body. Other symptoms may include fatigue, lethargy, swelling of the face or around the eyes, dry skin, decreased sweating, poor memory, hoarse voice, intolerance to cold and headache. Your doctor can give you a simple blood test if it is suspected you may suffer from this problem – as well as medicines to treat it.

Essential Fatty Acid Deficiency

Many people do not eat enough Essential Fatty Acids to provide their bodies with the amount it needs to carry out its role in hormone production and metabolic rate maintenance. Not only can this deficiency lead to problems with metabolism in itself but it can also lead the body to crave fatty foods. A craving which is then met with the wrong kinds of fat – and the wrong kinds of food. This deficiency can certainly be suspected as a culprit if you also suffer from dandruff or dry hair or skin. Best sources are salmon, flaxseed, walnuts and soy beans.

Food Sensitivity or Intolerance

Weight gain is common symptom of a food intolerance. See Eureka No. 40 for more details.

Cushing's Syndrome

Cushing's Syndrome is a disorder caused by an excess of the hormone cortisol. It is characterised in particular by fat accumulation around the face, abdomen and upper back. Ask your doctor if you research and then suspect this condition.

Prescription Drugs

Many prescription medicines can increase weight gain including HRT, oral contraceptives, steroids, nonsteroidal anti-inflammatory drugs (NSAIDs), antidepressants and diabetic medications. Discuss with your doctor before you take any action.

PCOS

As many as 10% of pre-menopausal women may suffer from polycystic ovary syndrome (PCOS) yet, despite the obvious symptoms, many fail to get diagnosed with it. At the bottom of PCOS is the fact that the ovaries and sometimes the adrenal glands are creating too much male hormone. Weight often starts increasing gradually after puberty or sometimes not 'till post-pregnancy. Other symptoms can include thinning hair, excess facial hair, severe acne, irregular periods and impaired fertility. Talk to your doctor if you think this could be your problem. You'd also be advised to do your own research on the internet.

Eating too much 'low-fat' food

This one, perhaps, should have come under 'eating to much carbohydrate' but it is sufficiently important in itself, I believe, to deserve its own heading. Whether it's strawberry cheesecake, macaroni cheese or Chicken Chop

Sui, you can now buy almost any kind of food your taste buds desire in the 'low fat' form. Unfortunately for your waistline, however, the promise of low-fat can actually mean piling on more pounds? Why? Because in many times out of 10, low-fat foods contain a high level of sweeteners, sugar and carbohydrates that can cause weight gain. They may also lead your body to crave more of the real and nutritionally rich food it really needs. Not to mention the fact that it's all adding to your uneasy relationship with real food itself.

Larger portion sizes

One of the biggest culprits in over-eating is the large portion sizes that we now consume. A study by the World Cancer Research Fund (WCRF), for example, found that burgers have doubled in size since 1980. You have also no doubt noticed the increase in the size of everything from packets of crisps and Mars bars to the fish and chips you get served in a restaurant.

Buy smaller plates. Put less on your plate and don't go back for seconds. Don't be afraid to leave some of what's on your plate. And make your portions gradually smaller and smaller for every year of your age.

A Summary of ALL the 47 Eurekas

And if we could summarise all the 47 Eurekas into one?

Go placidly amid the noise and thoughtfully through life

Do not just settle for what you currently have but continually look to make or do things better. Whether it's paying attention to the deep needs of your family or working towards more satisfaction in your working life, it's all too easy to stop when things are 'good enough'. Yet that extra bit of effort could make the difference between a life lived well enough and a life lived beautifully. A life that might inspire others to live better, a life that may make the world a better place.

Strip your mind of all the negative habits that create a shadow of anxiety and sadness in your life. Work on positive habits of thought that embrace a love for everything and a passion for life and this universe. Do not take in and absorb the negative events of your life but rather let them pass by you like storm clouds. Let go of pain and embrace happiness. Even if this means losing a part of who you think you are, then is that really such a bad thing?

Desiderata

Go placidly amid the noise and the haste,
and remember what peace there may be in silence.
As far as possible, without surrender,
be on good terms with all persons.
Speak your truth quietly and clearly;
and listen to others,
even to the dull and the ignorant;
they too have their story.
Avoid loud and aggressive persons;

they are vexatious to the spirit.
If you compare yourself with others,
you may become vain or bitter,
for always there will be greater and lesser persons than yourself.
Enjoy your achievements as well as your plans.
Keep interested in your own career, however humble;
it is a real possession in the changing fortunes of time.
Exercise caution in your business affairs,
for the world is full of trickery.
But let this not blind you to what virtue there is;
many persons strive for high ideals,
and everywhere life is full of heroism.
Be yourself. Especially do not feign affection.
Neither be cynical about love,
for in the face of all aridity and disenchantment,
it is as perennial as the grass.
Take kindly the counsel of the years,
gracefully surrendering the things of youth.
Nurture strength of spirit to shield you in sudden misfortune.
But do not distress yourself with dark imaginings.
Many fears are born of fatigue and loneliness.
Beyond a wholesome discipline,
be gentle with yourself.
You are a child of the universe
no less than the trees and the stars;
you have a right to be here.
And whether or not it is clear to you,
no doubt the universe is unfolding as it should.
Therefore be at peace with God,
whatever you conceive Him to be.
And whatever your labors and aspirations,
in the noisy confusion of life,
keep peace in your soul.
With all its sham, drudgery, and broken dreams,
it is still a beautiful world.
Be cheerful. Strive to be happy.

Max Ehrmann,
a poet and lawyer from Terre Haute, India

Get more Eureka thoughts and solutions like this –

FREE every week!

If you have enjoyed and benefited from the ideas in this book then I'd like to invite you to become a subscriber to my free online e-column, Life is a Bag of Revels.

Every week I send out a missive on a topic that can range from how to avoid a cold or make your kids successful… to the meaning of life or the truth about recession.

You can visit my website today and read some of my latest columns that include:

- The happiest country in the world: Why the recession will actually be good for us
- How to survive the winter: Colds, chilblains, chapped hands and charging up your batteries
- 5 Ways to boost your brain power and concentration
- 17 ways to make each moment of your day longer

It is totally free to sign up and you can unsubscribe at any time.

Visit **www.bagofrevels.co.uk**

Speak to you again soon

Wendy Churchill

Wendy Churchill